GREAT DAY HIKES

in
&
around *Napa Valley*

Vineyards and deep meadows,
islanded and framed with thicket,
gave place more and more as we ascended
to woods of oak and madrona,
dotted with enormous pines. . . .
A rough smack of resin was in the air,
and a crystal mountain purity.
It came pouring over these green slopes
by the oceanful.
The woods sang aloud,
and gave largely of their healthful breath.
Gladness seemed to inhabit these upper zones,
and we had left indifference
behind us in the valley.

— Robert Louis Stevenson,
The Silverado Squatters

GREAT DAY HIKES

in
&
around *Napa Valley*

KEN STANTON

BORED FEET PUBLICATIONS
MENDOCINO, CALIFORNIA
1997

© 1995, 1997 by Ken Stanton
First printing, September 1995
Second printing, July 1997
Printed in the United States of America

Photographs by Ken Stanton, except photo on page 38 reprinted by
    permission of Society of California Pioneers
Illustration of rattlesnake grass (*Briza maxima*) by Elizabeth
    Petersen
Maps by Bob Lorentzen,. Elizabeth Petersen, and USGS except
    maps on pages 51 and 120 by California Department of Parks
    and Recreation, and on page 106 by park staff, used by
    permission
Design by Elizabeth Petersen Graphic Design, Fort Bragg, CA
Edited by Nancy Kay Webb

Published by
Bored Feet Publications
Post Office Box 1832
Mendocino, California 95460
707-964-6629 / Fax: 707-964-5953

ALL RIGHTS RESERVED. No part of this book may be reproduced or transmitted in
any form or by any means, electronic or mechanical, including photocopying,
recording or by any information and retrieval system without written permission from
the author, except for the inclusion of brief quotations in a review.

Information contained in this book is correct to the best of the author's
knowledge at date of publication. Author and publisher assume no liability for
damages arising from errors or omissions. You must take the responsibility for your
safety and health while on these trails. Safety conditions of trails vary with seasons and
over time. Be cautious, assume that changes have occurred, heed the warnings in this
book and always check on local conditions. If these conditions are not satisfactory, you
may return this book unread for a full refund.

Library of Congress Cataloging-in-Publication Data
Stanton, Ken
    Great day hikes in and around Napa Valley/Ken Stanton.
        144 pp.
    Includes bibliographical references and index.
    ISBN 0-939431-20-3 : $12.00
    1. Hiking—California—Napa County—Guide-books. 2. Napa County
    (Calif.)—Description and travel—guide-books.   I. Title.

ISBN 0-939431-20-3

10 9 8 7 6 5 4 3 2

*Dedicated to all those who work selflessly
for open space in Napa County*

ACKNOWLEDGMENTS

In a book of this kind there are many people who play both large and small roles. I would like to thank all of them and those I have inadvertently omitted. Thanks go first of all to Clyde Weiss, Jo Maillard, Genji Schmeder and Ken Thatcher who know hiking trails in Napa intimately and pointed out many of the lesser known trails. My principal editor was Nancy Kay Webb, while John Hoffnagle, Joe Callizo and Bill Grummer also read and corrected the manuscript. Thanks to my publisher Bob Lorentzen and graphic artist Liz Petersen for making it easy to work together. Lucy Shaw and Reece Baswell provided the idea for this book. Mike Joell and Glen Mattila both gave their valuable time to hike Westwood Hills with me. Ellen Brannick and Mylon Pittman were essential sources for the Skyline Park chapter. Thanks to K.K. Burtis for her expertise on Native American history and Rod Broyles for trail updates at Bothe Park.

I was able to cover several days worth of work in an afternoon thanks to Donna Howard and her wonderful staff at the Lake County Museum. The Napa County Historical Society staff provided information for several chapters. Thanks to Jake Rugyt and Joe Callizo for their expertise on native plants. Also Jim Swanson and Teresa Le Blanc of California Department of Fish and Game for help on Cedar Roughs and Napa River Ecological Reserve. Greg Mangan and Scott Adams from the Bureau of Land Management helped me find the Blue Ridge trail. A special thanks to Bob McKenzie for his insights into life at Monticello and Berryessa Valley. Tom Klimowski and Roy Mason are in great part the Rockville Hills chapter. Dean Enderlin generously allowed us of his Trailside Geology of the Oat Hill Road.

In addition I'd like to acknowledge Sandi Frey of Lakeport Library, Bob Carlson and Sherry Stone of Napa Parks and Recreation, Glenn Burch and Marla Hastings of State Parks, Napa River project manager Bob Sorsen, Ann and Duane Smith of Solano Audubon, David Storck and Mike Sanford-Brown of the Petrified Forest, Tony Cerar, Helen Enos, Supervisors Mel Varrelman and Paul Batiste, Napa planning director John Yost, Kevin Williams, Barbara Stafford, Gina Urbani, Barbara Pahre, Ed Reynolds, Earl Balch and Dave Briggs.

CONTENTS

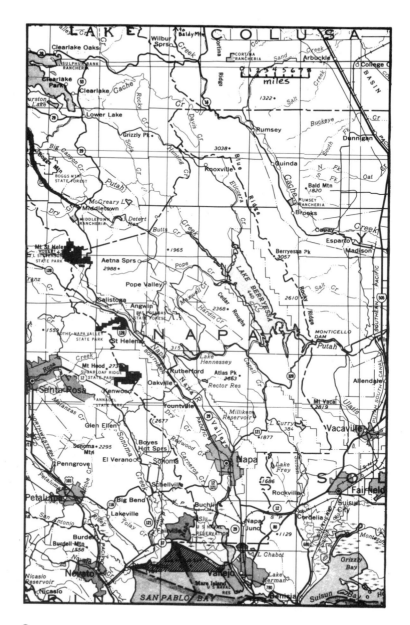

8

INTRODUCTION

Twenty years ago I was an idealist. Although an active hiker and climber, I owned no guide books nor wanted any. For me, a guidebook was an obstacle to the pure outdoor experience. Unfettered with someone else's thoughts, I could experience the wilderness on my own terms. Not that I wasn't prepared. All the necessities for a safe trip were stowed in the old Kelty, but the load was light. I took the minimalist approach, no camera, no flashlight, no tent and certainly no guide book.

At last shelf count, not including the ones lost or permanently loaned, my hiking, climbing and international travel guide books numbered fifty-two.

Times changed and so did I. When the National Park Service began quotas for heavily traveled areas of the Sierra Nevada in the 1970s, I balked. A High Sierra bureaucracy seemed like an oxymoron. I wanted to go wherever and whenever it suited me. Today the wisdom of their decision is obvious. No place is an island and resource management, including quotas, is an imperative.

I still struggle, though, with the guidebook issue. "Won't a hiking guide increase traffic and diminish the solitude you seek?" people ask. Yes, but many actions we take are two-edged. John Muir struggled with the same issue. The father of the conservation movement would rather have spent his time outdoors than at his writing desk. Muir once wrote that after spending some time in the city, he returned to Yosemite, where he took the only serious fall of his career, knocking him unconscious. His reprimand to himself: "That is what you get by intercourse with stupid town stairs and dead pavements."

Yet he chose to write of Yosemite for a world audience, pleading for its preservation, knowing only wide spread public support could save it. No one doubts the wisdom of his decision, despite the three million visitors a year who threaten to love it to death. That is a problem for our generation to deal with.

Although most Napa natives prefer to keep their own trails to themselves, the reality is that for at least twenty-five years, visitors have accounted for fifty percent of outdoor recreation in Napa County. Unless population reaches stasis, that figure will increase. That is bad news for some locals. But it can be good news too. The more people know and love these hills, the stronger the efforts to save them from development.

The Oat Hill Mine Trail is a case in point. The old freight wagon road near Calistoga, closed to vehicles since 1979, is so rich in historical, geological and botanical wonders that it wins my vote as the finest hiking trail in this guide. Landowner/developers posed a serious threat in 1990 when they illegally attempted to bulldoze and widen the road. This was a first step in their proposal to place a dozen multimillion dollar ranchettes on oak-studded hilltops overlooking Calistoga. The attempt was stopped but a subsequent alternate access was illegally cut. While state and local officials attempt to gain preservation status for the trail, the threat remains very real.

One of the higher purposes of a guide is to inform and seek support for worthy causes such as this. Other areas of concern are Napa's two state parks: Bothe-Napa Valley and Robert Louis Stevenson. Due to California budget constraints, fewer rangers must deal with more visitors each year. Administrators are seeking creative funding solutions, but, for example, at Bothe Park only volunteer effort allows the visitors' center to stay open. At Robert Louis Stevenson State Park, already grossly underutilized, rangers are now hard pressed to make weekend patrols. This leaves responsibility more and more in the hands of the public. The situation seems to point increasingly to the private sector — for volunteers, and for financial and moral support.

Why in the world has there been no hiking guide to Napa County until now? The answer seems obvious — Napa is wine country, not a hiking destination. Even as this guide was planned, the doubts remained. Could I find enough material to fill a book? Many of the hikes originally seen as likely candidates were eliminated, and usually for one reason — lack of full public access.

Napa County was once a quiet, drowsy backwoods, where prunes and walnuts were as common as the grape. Most of the hillsides were, even then, private property, but access was easier. You just let your neighbor know you were taking the mare for a ride, and closed the gate behind you. Starting in the mid 1960s, the success of wine led to a new population influx. Hillside vineyards replaced fir forests and chaparral slopes, and every wealthy San Franciscan wanted a chateau on forty acres overlooking Napa Valley. Beginning in the 1970s, property owners' growing fear of lawsuits led to fences, signs, and closures. Suddenly, land accessible for decades was off limits. There are probably few serious hikers today who can honestly say they've never done a bit of discreet trespassing. But this kind of thing cannot be advocated nor work as a solution.

It is a curious fact that in Napa, not a single county-owned-and-operated park exists. The county was way ahead of its time in 1968 when it established the revolutionary agricultural preserve, which has single-handedly prevented Napa from becoming another bedroom community of the Bay Area. Napans have since expressed further support for this concept by passing Measure J, extending the preserve to the year 2020.

Yet Napa County is equally far behind in supplying bona fide recreational access to its citizens. In 1974 a county-appointed committee was asked to address this issue. Their 150 page report, critical of the county, was as visionary in its concept and recommendations as was the agricultural preserve. This report, called *Napa County's Park and Recreation Plan*, was never adopted due to lack of public support. Twenty years later almost all of the plan's major components which have become reality are those implemented by other agencies.

Napa County's Park and Recreation Plan was submitted in March 1976 after two years of work, including consultation with local agencies and numerous public hearings. The committee was quick to point out that, "In contrast to almost all other California counties, Napa County at present time does not budget money on a regular basis for the creation, operation, and maintenance of Park or Recreation areas and facilities at the county level." They also made it clear that "the county has the basic responsibility among local governments for the preparation, adoption, and maintenance of a countywide parks and recreation plan."

The basic elements of the plan were:

1) Development of county parks on land in public ownership;
2) A system of county scenic roads;
3) A system of riding and hiking trails to connect with all county, state and federal recreation areas;
4) Bicycle routes using public road rights-of-way (Southern Pacific Railroad track line considered a desirable route separated from the roadway); and
5) Rest areas.

Highest on their list of priorities for county parks was

Skyline County Park, followed by Valley Oak County Park (Napa Valley Ecological Reserve) and Lake Hennessey Recreation Area. Alternate suggestions included the 2,232-acre Milliken Reservoir area and the 5,200-acre Rector Reservoir area, both in public lands.

The most far-reaching and exciting idea in the plan was called the Napa Crest Trail. The committee envisioned a one hundred-mile loop trail for hikers and horseback riders, following the eastern and western ridge lines of Napa Valley from Napa to Mount St. Helena. Connector trails would hook up with all park and recreation areas, public and private. For example, a hiker could start at Bothe-Napa Valley State Park, connect with the Napa Crest Trail and finish at Sugarloaf Ridge State Park in Sonoma County. They also proposed cross-valley trails and designated one day loop trails.

What has happened in the twenty years since this remarkable proposal? Skyline Wilderness Park became a reality in 1983 with the county playing a minor role. At the public's urging, the state-owned land was leased to the county, which in turn leases it to Skyline Park Citizens Association, a private group operating the park today. Napa Valley Ecological Reserve was born when the state purchased the development-threatened property and turned it over to Fish and Game for management. Lake Hennessey is still owned by the City of Napa with limited boating and walking access. Proposed day-use camps and trails on the lake's east side were not developed. The Napa Crest Trail has been the biggest disappointment. Very little else from the Plan has been implemented. The county has long maintained it has no wish to be in the park management business. Although it endorses the concept of recreational access, the voting public has balked. In 1992 a ballot measure for an Open Space District was turned down by the voters of Napa County.

The City of Napa, on the other hand, has nearly forty regional, community and neighborhood parks. It also has begun a system of trails that will interconnect with two larger trails now in the development stage, the Bay Trail and the Bay Area Ridge Trail. The Bay Trail is a 400 mile multi-use path that will circle San Francisco and San Pablo Bays. Currently one third finished, it will connect nine bay area counties and forty-two shoreline cities. It dovetails with the city's Napa River Trail at John F. Kennedy Park.

Also passing through Napa is the Bay Area Ridge Trail, first conceived in the 1960s by visionary conservationist, the late William Penn Mott. The Bay Area Ridge Trail Council is a grassroots organization that seeks to complete the 400-mile trail that would follow the mountains encircling the greater Bay Area. As of this writing, nearly 180 miles are dedicated. Four of those miles follow Skyline Trail in Skyline Wilderness Park.

A third proposal, the Napa Valley Trail, would start at Cutting's Wharf, connecting with the Napa River Trail, and continuing along the length of the river to its source at Mount St. Helena. Due to intense rural and urban land use, implementing this trail would be difficult.

Earlier, the question arose, would there be sufficient material to fill a Napa hiking guide? The answer of course is yes. Even after pursuing county trails for fifteen years, I was delighted to find many that were new to me. I'm confident most readers will discover opportunities they weren't aware of before.

Great Day Hikes in and around Napa Valley describes nearly one hundred miles of trails, many never before published. They range from casual walks suitable for small children, to endurance contests fit for a Tibetan sherpa. Some of these hikes, in state and city parks, will be known by many locals. Others, on state- or federally-owned land or on easements through private land, you could drive past without knowing they exist. Most of the trails are in Napa County. For those feeling a need to "step out", I included one hike in each of the adjoining counties of Sonoma, Lake,

Yolo, and two in Solano.

Napa Valley lies in a climatic transition zone between the cool moist air of the coast and the warm dry air of the Central Valley. The Mayacmas Mountains on the west are wetter and more wooded, suitable for hiking in summer and fall. On the east the Vaca Mountains are drier and exposed to the sun, making them a good winter and spring destination. The best seasons to hike in Napa County are spring and fall, with many fine days between storms in winter. Summer is often too warm.

WINTER is a great season to hike if you are properly prepared, with extra clothes and rain gear in your pack. The trails are quiet, the air clear, and views from ridgetops outstanding. On the coldest days, with the wind chill near freezing, a thermos of hot tea or coffee is miraculous for the spirits. If it's a decision between a thermos of steaming liquid and my big telephoto lens, I bring the thermos every time. When the dreaded tule fogs slink in for an extended

Lake Berryessa

stay, and the valley is dank and miserable, the ridgetops can be bathed in glorious sunshine. Recommended hikes: Oat Hill Mine Trail, Rim Rock Trail in Skyline Park, Mount St. Helena, Lake Hennessey.

SPRING is the most pleasant and rewarding season. Temperatures are moderate, the hills are green, and rains have brought wildflowers. On many warm days short pants and short sleeve shirts can be worn, but keep extra clothes in the pack for sudden weather changes. In stable weather, fogs will push in from the coast and cover the valley until late morning. You'll be in the sun in the hills above 1,000 feet or so. Recommended hikes: Oat Hill Mine Trail, Skyline Trail, Blue Ridge, Rockville Hills, Sugarloaf Park, Westwood Hills, Mount St. Helena, Baldy Mountain.

SUMMER can be the least desirable time in Napa. The air is hazy, temperatures high, grasses and watercourses have turned dry. Notwithstanding, there are good options. Try early morning and evening, or even moonlight hiking. Choose the shady creek trails on the valley's west side or Skyline Park. Bring water, a hat, sunscreen and forget the rain gear. Watch for the appearance of fog, it means cooler temperatures for a few days. Recommended hikes: Redwood and Ritchey Canyon Trails in Bothe Park, Marie Creek Trail in Skyline, Napa Valley Ecological Reserve.

FALL is a beautiful time in the valley. The weather is often stable, morning air is crisp, and deciduous trees and vines turn color. The yellows, reds, and pinks of black oak, sycamore, and dogwood leaves make a brilliant contrast to the dominant evergreen forest. Shorts and tee shirts are appropriate wear as late as Halloween. Recommended hikes: Petrified Forest, Buckeye and Lake Marie Trails at Skyline, Coyote Peak at Bothe, Stebbins Cold Canyon Reserve.

Note: Weather extremes can be severe at Baldy Mountain, Blue Ridge and Mount St. Helena.

MOUNT SAINT HELENA

Robert Louis Stevenson State Park is Napa's largest

DIRECTIONS: From Calistoga, drive north on Highway 29 almost 8 miles until signs indicate you have arrived at Robert Louis Stevenson State Park. There are parking lots on either side of the road. The trail begins on the west side.

DISTANCE: 5 miles one way

GRADE: Strenuous

ELEVATION GAIN: 2,100 feet

BEST TIME: Spring, fall. Once or twice a winter snows provide fun for snowshoers, skiers, and kamikaze mountain bikers.

INFO: Bothe-Napa Valley State Park, 707/942-4575

FACILITIES: Several picnic tables. Find water 2 miles north on Highway 29 at Rattlesnake Spring.

Kana'mota was the Wappo Indian name for Mount St. Helena, meaning human mountain. For thousands of years, Kana'mota was the geographical and spiritual heart of Wappo land. The Wappo tell the story of Coyote and his grandson Chicken Hawk, who, with his two sisters, flies to the dry top of Kana'mota when it rains for twenty days and nights. All others are drowned by the flood waters. When the waters recede, Coyote rebuilds each house, places a feather there for each person, and brings gifts of speech, movement, laughter, and food from the Moon so they may live again. The mountain remains today a spiritual center and place of prayer for the Wappo people.

The Mexican period in northern California was short but influential. The Franciscans founded the last of the missions in Sonoma in 1823. As the story goes, when Father Jose Altimira saw the great mountain to the north, its summit in profile reminded him of a saint's tomb he had seen in an abbey in Rheims, France. He named it for Helena, mother of Constantine the Great.

The Mexican government was fearful of the Russian colony at Fort Ross. In an effort to prevent Russian expansion, they began in the 1830s to grant land to trusted individuals. These Mexican land grants were given to Mexican citizens or Americans who changed citizenship. In 1839 Dr. Edward Bale was given *Rancho Carne Humana*, one of the largest land grants in Napa County, stretching from mid-valley to the foot of Mount St. Helena. At the southern and western base of Mount St. Helena was Rancho Mallacomas (*Moristul y Plan de Agua Caliente*), given to Jose Berryessa in 1843.

The Mexican expansion played only a small part in the Russians' decision to leave. Crop failure and depletion of the sea otters had made Fort Ross an economic failure. Before they left in 1841, scientist Il'ia Voznesenski made a final expedition into the interior to conduct botanical and ethnographic studies. With his companion Chernykh they made the first recorded ascent of the tallest peak in the region, leaving a copper plaque affixed to a rock at the summit. Like Father Altimira, they also christened the peak Mount Saint Helena. Back home in Saint Petersburg, Voznesenski would spend the rest of his life cataloguing his remarkable collection.

The same year the Mexican government bid farewell to the Russians, the Bidwell-Bartleson Party crested the Sierra Nevada. A whole new problem had arrived. Overland par-

Mt. St. Helena viewed from Oat Hill Mine Trail

ties of American settlers slowly settled the Napa Valley in the 1840s. Following the Bear Flag Revolt, California became part of the United States in 1846. The Mexican land grants, if not tied up in court over property disputes, were parceled and sold to the newcomers. After the gold rush of 1849, Napa Valley quickly filled with Americans.

In 1850 the Bull Trail was carved out of the woods by volunteer effort. It followed an Indian trail from Calistoga to Middletown. This steep, narrow grade was the official road for eighteen years. Cattle and hogs, sometimes hauling sleds, were driven to market from Lake County, but it was too rugged for wheeled vehicles.

Miners meanwhile kept the gold fever alive by prospecting in the hills. They finally found their own El Dorado in the form of cinnabar over near Pope Valley in 1861. Cinnabar's by-product, quicksilver, was in heavy demand for gold refining in Nevada. Shipments increased through the 1860s until entrepreneur John Lawley saw his cue. Knowing the railroad was coming to Calistoga, he built a new road over the mountain to connect the mines with the railhead. Lawley's Toll Road was finished in 1868, designed and maintained with the mines' freight wagon traffic in mind. He and his family would collect toll at the top of the grade for more than half a century.

The last quarter of the nineteenth century was the golden age for Napa County's mining industry. Mines like the Redington in Knoxville, the Aetna and Oat Hill near Pope Valley, and the Mirabel and Great Western on Mount St. Helena made this area the second richest quicksilver strike in United States history. Gold and silver were also found, at the Silverado Mine on Mount St. Helena and at the Palisades Mine near Calistoga.

A spinoff 'industry' developed as a result of mining's success: road agentry. Stagecoaches loaded with payroll for the mines were often robbed by highwaymen on the Lawley Road. Quite often they were amateurs who needed some extra cash. Commonly they were friends or acquaintances. As historian Anne Roller Issler has said, "Like deer on the mountain, stage robbers were neighbors until they became game."

Others, like Lake County resident Buck English, made a career of stage robbing. Buck was in and out of jail most of his adult life for cattle rustling, stagecoach heists and various other crimes. In 1895 his last robbery took place on Lawley's Toll Road near the Mountain Mill House, and led to the most exciting manhunt in Napa County history. He escaped with $1,000 and disappeared for three days, wearing out his shoes traveling the rugged Oat Hill country. He was finally apprehended on the Mount George Grade near Napa after a wild shootout. San Quentin's prisoner number 16426 spent most of his remaining years behind bars.

The greatest period of gold and silver mining came to an end around the turn of the century. After 1900, quicksilver mines began a slow decline. Horse-drawn wagons now had to share the road (unwillingly) with the automobile. As the highwayman disappeared, stagecoaches stopped carrying firearms by 1910. By 1915 horse-drawn stages were replaced by auto buses. Around this time Mount St. Helena's other toll road, the Ida Clayton, went public. Increasing public pressure and falling revenues forced Mollie Patten, John Lawley's daughter, to sell the Lawley Toll Road to the state. By 1924 the new highway left Mollie and the Toll House by the wayside. An era had passed.

The last major road on the mountain was built in 1935. E.A. Erickson was state forest ranger based at Las Posadas Forest in Angwin. He successfully lobbied Sacramento for a lookout tower on Mount St. Helena, and for a fire road to the summit. Just as the Civilian Conservation Corps was finishing the fire road, they were called away suddenly without expecting to return. Ignoring the carefully placed survey markers, the last quarter mile was bulldozed in a hurry, straight uphill.

Public access lands and resorts have been on the rise from the 1930s to the present. It started with trout farms like Smith's off the Ida Clayton Road and Russel's in Troutdale Canyon. Later the old Silverado mining town site became a dude ranch offering horseback rides to the summit. Girl Scouts ran a camp near the Mountain Mill House. The most significant change came in 1949 when Norman Livermore gave the first forty acres of land for budding Robert Louis Stevenson Memorial Park. It has enlarged over the years to 3,760 acres. The Department of Parks improved the trail to the monument and connected it with the fire road, now the main route to the summit.

For well over a hundred years a trail of one sort or another has cleaved the brush and skirted the volcanic outcrops to the top. C.A. Menefee's history of Napa, Lake, Sonoma and Mendocino counties in 1873 states that "a good trail has been made for the accommodation of tourists which renders the ascent easy." Whether ten miles of trail are ever easy depends on your condition, but another of his statements gives one pause: "Towards the north, Clear Lake lies mapped out in plain view." Today only summits surrounding the lake, like Mount Konocti, are visible. Whether

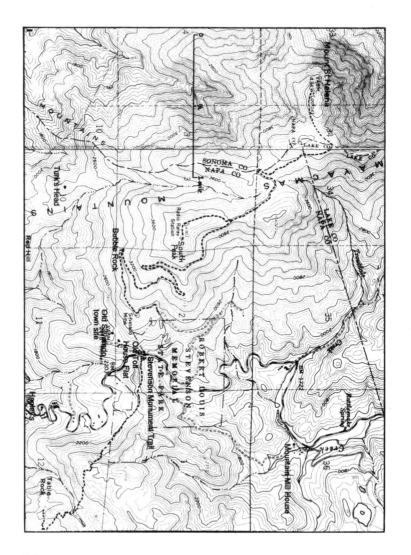

22

Menefee made the ascent or not, it's clear that Mount St. Helena has one of the oldest recreational trails in the county.

Table Rock, a part of the spectacular Palisades, was included in the state park in 1993. State officials and local interest groups are currently working on a plan for all the Palisades to be part of Robert Louis Stevenson State Park one day. The plan includes the Oat Hill Mine Trail. If all goes well, this would be the finest hiking trail in Napa County.

TRAIL NOTES:

From the west parking lot, wooden steps lead to a large pleasant clearing. Lawley's Toll House stood against the hillside; some of its foundation is still there. The stage-coaches would pass right in front, after they paid toll and Mollie Patten lifted the gate. A remnant of the original road can be traced from the clearing's north end to the present highway. Picnic tables are scattered around the site of an old croquet ground, also used as a bocce ball court before World War II.

At the trail sign, the path immediately leads into a mixed evergreen forest of madrone, black oak, Douglas fir, tan oak and bay. Easy switchbacks lead up the steep hill for more than ½ mile. Then the forest thins as manzanita and knobcone pine appear. At the last switchback stop for a view of the Palisades to the southeast, then descend to the granite marker commemorating Robert Louis Stevenson's honeymoon visit in the summer of 1880. At that time the clearing was open enough for a view of Napa Valley. All the Douglas fir on the mine tailings flat beside the monument are probably post mine-closure age, that is, 1877 or later. Stevenson took notes that summer for *The Silverado Squatters*, one of his minor works but still the best book written about Napa Valley.

The upper shaft of the Silverado Mine is uphill to the left. This is an intriguing place to explore but be aware — a significant amount of rock has fallen here in recent years. One climber dislodged a one ton boulder from the seventy-five-foot north face in 1993. Missing his rope by inches, it split in two on impact and careened downhill to the monument flat. Fortunately no one was hurt.

The roughest part of the 5-mile trail leads past the monument to the fire road at ⅞ mile. Along this segment you leave the seclusion of shady fir forest and enter the bright, sunlit world of chaparral and stubby knobcone pine. At mile 1 you are directly above the upper mine shaft and looking straight down the Napa Valley. If it's not smoggy, foggy or hazy you'll see the twin-summited peak of Mount Diablo sixty-six miles south. The fire-tested south-facing slopes stretching before you support eight species of manzanita, plus chamise, ceanothus, toyon, coffeeberry and mountain mahogany. The best spring flower displays are seen along here: bush poppies, chaparral pea, Indian warrior and monkeyflower.

In ¼ mile you pass a gathering of gray pine, bay, and canyon live oak that somehow escaped the last century of fires. Beyond is the Bubble Rock. Hikers get a kick out of watching climbers scale the vertical and overhanging pocket ladders. In this area are many more fantastically shaped pillars of old lava and ash flow of varying degrees of reliability. The most solid of these crags are now considered some of the best rock climbing in the Bay Area.

The road ahead will turn rocky in places but generally reflects the wishes of the road builders who wanted an easy grade to carry materials for the summit lookout tower. As you climb you'll see Blue Ridge to the east, the prominent backbone of the Vaca Mountains that separates the North Coast Ranges from the Central Valley. The Sierra will also be visible on a clear day.

At a big switchback at 2¼ miles, look for 7,056-foot Snow Mountain in the southern portion of Mendocino National Forest. The massive bulk of Mount St. Helena's south peak shades your trail until a trail junction at 3¼ miles. Here a partially paved trail, slightly shorter than ½ mile, leads to the 4,003 foot top of the south peak. In 1987 Telecommunications Incorporated built an observation deck with a display showing air line miles to various regional peaks. The topmost forty acres is an inholding of the Bureau of Land Management, which leases the land to companies owning communications equipment. This is a satisfying destination for many hikers. Views are excellent to the south, east and west.

Cross the flat, so-callesd summit plateau once erroneously described in the 1873 *Bancroft's Tourist Guide to Napa Valley* as the crater of the extinct volcano. Almost imperceptibly you pass over the headwaters of Kimball Creek at 3¾ miles. It leads to the city of Calistoga's municipal water supply at the foot of Kimball Canyon. Start to climb again at mile 4. Look for giant chinquapin and sniff for the sickly sweet smell of tobacco brush. The waters of Lake Berryessa are now visible below Berryessa Peak.

At 4½ miles a junction leads to one of the middle peaks. The 100-foot microwave

Fiddleheads announce the arrival of spring

tower recently installed leaves one aghast. Soon you arrive at Windy Point and the first view of the Geysers' white plumes. The few sugar pines around provide welcome sun relief. The last ¼ mile is steep. You will pass the rare Rincon Ridge Buckbrush, a mound-forming ceanothus up to eighteen inches high, found only on this mountain and near Santa Rosa.

Your climb ends after 5 miles at the 4,339-foot summit (the official height was lowered four feet by USGS researchers in 1994). Both the middle and north peaks are part of a 200-acre inholding of the Livermore family. California Division of Forestry leases the site for the lookout tower, which remains unmanned in 1995 due to budget cuts. Look closely behind the tower for an exact replica of the Russian plaque marking the first ascent in 1841. Words are written in English and Russian for you bilingual hikers.

The summit slopes gently west to what the State Mineralogist tagged the Giant's Causeway in 1885. This is the top of columnar andesite cliffs that buttress the north peak. Notice the five-sided jointing similar to Devil's Postpile in the eastern Sierra. The steep north slopes drop into remote Rattlesnake and Bradford canyons where black bear, bobcat, fox and mountain lion roam. From here views can be breathtaking of the Pacific Ocean, San Francisco and Sierra summits. You might also see California's share of the Cascade Range, Mounts Lassen and Shasta, the latter 192 miles distant.

TABLE ROCK

DISTANCE: 2½ miles one way
GRADE: Moderate
BEST TIME: Winter, spring
DIRECTIONS: The unsigned trail begins at the east parking lot across the highway from the Mount St. Helena trailhead.

TRAIL NOTES:

Ascend switchbacks through a cool forest of tan oak, maple, bay and Douglas fir for several hundred feet until turning left onto a road. At ½ mile Snow Mountain will be visible to the north on clear days. Resume climbing at a notch around ⅝ mile, leaving the highway behind.

Take the right fork at ¾ mile and the road soon turns to trail. Beyond 1⅛ miles you pass the former park boundary prior to the Table Rock purchase of 1993. Great views of Bear and Cub valleys appear. The trail turns sharply right, then before a prominent rock outcrop it dives down and left. Exercise caution on a steep, loose section until leveling out at a flat.

Let the curving row of rocks lead you to an opening in the brush at 1½ miles. Soon a second, steeper and looser descent follows. Continue descending through grasses until you reach an idyllic spot on tiny Garnett Creek before 2¼ miles. Cross the stream and start climbing again through forest. Soon you come out among fantastic volcanic formations. The trail is picturesque here, especially if the little tributary is running.

At 2½ miles turn to the right (west) and walk toward a tableland of volcanics. **EXERCISE EXTREME CAUTION** as you approach the edge of Table Rock, which drops off sheer for 200 feet. Return the same way.

OAT HILL MINE TRAIL

Old freight wagon road leads into the past

DIRECTIONS: Follow Highway 29 or Silverado Trail north until the two roads meet, .5 mile north of Calistoga. Park alongside either road or Lake Street, but avoid the small dirt lot at the trailhead. The trail begins at the metal gate.

DISTANCE: 4⅞ miles one way

GRADE: Strenuous

ELEVATION GAIN: 1,900 feet

BEST TIME: Spring

WARNINGS: Status of the trail is uncertain at this time. Please stay on the trail to avoid trespassing on private property. Let's not jeopardize current efforts to bring this marvelous trail into the state park system.

The Oat Hill Mine Road might never have become an important thoroughfare of Napa County without the Pope Valley mining boom of the late 1800s. There are too many other stream valleys and low mountain passes to follow without the rocky and precipitous contours of the Palisades to deal with. Even with the heavy demand for the road, it took three separate attempts over twenty years to finally complete.

In 1861 John Newman was on a hunting trip near Aetna Springs when out of curiosity he picked up a rock. It was cinnabar (from which mercury or quicksilver is made), and by the next year he and John Lawley would form the Phoenix Mining Company, the first in Napa County. Others would follow — the Washington, Corona, Twin Peaks, Red Hill, Silver Bow.

The railhead was brought to Calistoga by Sam Brannan in 1868, the same year John Lawley built his toll road over Mount St. Helena. Freight wagons carrying ore from these mines made the laborious trip to Butts Canyon Road into Middletown, and over the toll road to Calistoga. Mining companies paid heavy fees for the privilege of using Lawley's road.

In 1872 cinnabar was found at the base of Oat Hill. It would be years before the mine was ready for production. However, over by Knoxville at the northeast end of Napa County, the Redington Mine was the county's biggest producer. The owners petitioned the county for a road from Calistoga, over the Palisades, past the Phoenix Mine to the Redington. Construction was begun in 1873 but halted before all was finished.

Today we can only speculate about the reasons for the halt. Funds may have run short, or perhaps enough of the road was completed to serve the company's needs. Lack of demand may also have been a factor. By 1876 when a second attempt was made to finish it, the price per flask of quicksilver had dropped from more than a hundred dollars to forty-four dollars, primarily due to overproduction.

Then in 1880 John Lawley built another road from the Pope Valley mines to join Lawley's Toll Road at the Mountain Mill House. Today called the Livermore Road, it saved teamsters fourteen grueling miles. That same year the Oat Hill Mine, producing by 1876, had outpaced the Redington. The Oat Hill was on its way to becoming the sixth largest quicksilver mine in the world. At first owned by local men, it was bought by an outfit in Boston and became the Napa

Site of Flynn Homestead

Consolidated Company in the late 1870s.

As annual production rose at Napa Consolidated Mine, more profits were eaten up by toll road fees. Demand grew for a free and direct route to Calistoga. Napa Consolidated won the bidding to build the Calistoga/Oat Hill road for the county in 1892. Supervisor Newcomb then subcontracted the job to J.L. Priest of Chiles Valley. The rocky pass over the Palisades required blasting with dynamite, but apparently even the death of poor Priest did not delay completion of this segment that had stymied builders for twenty years. His brothers, William and Daniel Priest, finished the job by the contract date of June 1, 1893.

Even before completion, there were settlers on both sides of the Oat Hill Road. Irishman Patrick Flynn applied for and patented three homesteads on the Calistoga side, all within two miles of town. Just above the third and highest site, Flynn had a mining claim called the Leopard. He enjoyed the slow pace of traffic on the uncompleted Oat Hill, so in 1893 he was disgruntled when all the freight wagons began rumbling by. Flynn put up a gate with a lock, which the sheriff was obliged to cut. At the report of a second lock on the gate, the sheriff was not so amused. A stiff warning for Flynn's arrest kept the road open after that. After Flynn died, his daughter Mamie lived on their land into the 1930s.

With the completion of the Oat Hill Mine Road, a retired Finnish ship carpenter named Karl Holm was able to homestead 160 acres at the high point of the road. In 1898, in a beautiful grove of trees under the ramparts of the Palisades, he built a stone house, a barn and planted an orchard inside a stone wall. Springs from under the Palisades provided water. By the next year his neighbor John Holm (probably his brother) also owned 160 acres. John Holm died in February 1902; his widow, Kristina, married Karl later the same year.

John's children lost their homestead in 1906 for nonpayment of property taxes totalling less than five dollars. Karl and Kristina lost their place in 1910 for delinquent property taxes and a small loan default. According to Anthony Cerar, who lived at the Oat Hill Mine in those days, a German named Sperling lived at the site until his death in 1919.

The Oat Hill Mine was worked continuously until 1909 employing sixty whites and 120 Chinese. A town built up around it with families living in houses that covered the nearby hillsides. Oat Hill had its own general store, drug store, sawmill, slaughter house, blacksmith shop, post office, two boarding houses and a public school. It was here that Anthony Cerar went for three years of his education. He says the Calistoga road, as it was known to people on the Oat Hill side, was the only way to town until 1924. People of average means couldn't afford the Lawley Toll Road until it went public. He remembers watering troughs for freight wagon horses located at Flynn's, Holm's, Maple Springs, Corona Mine and the Oat Hill Mine. Cerar likes to tell anyone who listens that contemporary names for the Holm's place like China Camp and the Halfway House are false — "modern Hollywood fiction." There never was any such place.

With the gradual decline of the Pope Valley mines,

31

vehicle traffic thinned. There were good, faster and easier alternatives via Howell Mountain Road and Highway 29. A quietude descended on the Oat Hill Road in the 1930s and 1940s. Emphasis turned to occasional recreational use by hunters on foot or horseback who wished to reach the backcountry. After World War II a new era of use emerged when the commercial manufacture of the jeep brought four-wheelers to challenge the grade.

By the 1970s the long-unmaintained Oat Hill was a serious challenge for a jeep. Enthusiasts called it the "best little four-wheelin' road in the state." Local jeep clubs made regular pilgrimages in long caravans from Calistoga to Aetna Springs or Oat Hill. They often did maintainance on the road. Trouble came mostly from those who were unfamiliar with the road and/or intoxicated. Several people were injured and killed at this time, usually on the exposed last rocky mile to the pass.

One of these accidents in 1973 involved a young man and woman and their infant child. The vehicle plunged 300 yards, turning over several times, killing the couple. The child was discovered hours later in good condition, still strapped to his jump seat about seventy-five feet from the wreckage. Accidents like these brought up liability issues for the county of Napa. After a number of hearings, the Board of Supervisors formally closed and abandoned the road in 1979.

This was seen as good news by preservationists, who ten years earlier had formed the Palisades/Swartz Canyon Project Committee. With Harry Tranmer as chairman, they envisioned the Palisades, including the Oat Hill Mine Road, as one day a part of Robert Louis Stevenson State Park. In 1969, 120 acres of land at the pass belonging to the Duff family was transferred to the Nature Conservancy, giving conservationists a legal foothold. This now belongs to the Napa County Land Trust which grants public easement to the property. A 1988 bond act allowed the state to purchase the Table Rock property in 1993. Part of the dream had come to pass after twenty-five years. But even as local interests and state officials sought to use remaining funds for key land purchases, developers threatened to squash the dream.

Owners of a large parcel that includes Patrick Flynn's old homesteads proposed paving the Oat Hill Road and placing multimillion dollar ranchettes on hilltops. They

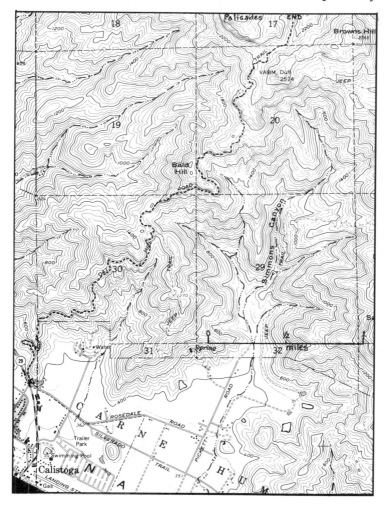

attempted to regrade the road but were stopped by a vigilant Genji Schmeder, local Sierra Club leader. Undeterred, developers bought an easement to the north and in 1992 illegally bulldozed one and a half miles of road adjoining the Oat Hill Road. They did it without permit and without an erosion control plan, in flagrant violation of Napa County's Hillside Ordinance. The Board of Supervisors gave them a $5,000 fine, a mere slap on the wrist. Recommendations to remove the road and restore it to its natural state were not implemented.

In response to this threat the Oat Hill Mine Trail Committee was born as a watchdog agency and advocate for the historic trail. It seeks to preserve the trail in its present state, and permanently protect it as a state park. Constant community vigilance and support are needed to prevent development that would surely destroy this area.

Today, the Oat Hill Mine Trail is a locally popular hiking route, with over 6,000 visitors a year. There may be no other like it in the world. Its unique geological and historical resources and obvious beauty make it richly deserving of preservation status. Efforts by many concerned people are helping to make this trail one to be enjoyed today and forever. You can join the cause by contacting the Oat Hill Mine Trail Committee, a part of Napa County Sierra Club, at P.O. Box 644, Napa, California 94559.

TRAIL NOTES*:

The hillside washout with the fence poised dramatically over it typifies the unstable soil encountered in the first ½ mile. The wide mix of trees include black oak, gray pine, toyon, scrub oak, and manzanita. Soon, Traulsen Vineyards appear downslope to the your left. All of their acclaimed zinfandel is grown on this two-acre estate. Silver dollar

* Geological information is taken from "Trailside Geology of the Oat Hill Road" by Dean Enderlin.

eucalyptus grows along the fence.

To your right is an old shale pit, actually weathered andesite lava. Similar rock ½ mile away was quarried for road base on Highway 29. Sign in at the trail register before ¼ mile. Data is monitored weekly by the Oat Hill Mine Trail Committee. Pass one of the worst slope washouts on the trail. Here you get an idea of the wildflowers the Oat Hill Road offers in the spring: brodiaea, fiddlenecks, buttercups, poppies and bush lupine. Watch for giant poison oak bushes at the big switchback.

At ½ mile you see the worst slide of the 1995 flood, which stopped just short of taking out the trail. From here you soon enter rhyolite lava flows that occurred in the last stage of the Sonoma Volcanic field, about three million years ago. The trail now faithfully follows the contours of the hills, meandering alternately into the shady stream canyons, and out into the grassy meadows. You'll find the road builders one hundred years ago did a beautiful job. In places the trail seems too narrow to have accommodated freight wagons. Plant growth and some erosion have obscured the original width.

At mile 1 you can look straight down Lincoln Avenue, the main street of Calistoga. In another ⅜ mile is a clearing with large Douglas firs. Groupings of Indian warrior show here every spring.

A curious unit of rock around 1¾ miles confused earlier geologists into mapping it as sandstone. This fine-grained, white-to-tan-colored tuff fell as ash into an ancient lake during volcanic eruptions. Fossils are often found in such water-lain rock, but not here. Violent volcanic eruptions of the time had virtually eliminated all plant and animal life.

You pass a large meadow where Mamie Flynn lived alone in a cabin. She got her water from the creek nearby in spring, but in summer she walked to town and carried it back in gallon jugs.

Just up the trail Mamie's father, Patrick Flynn, worked

a mining claim from 1889 to 1907. He drove a crosscut one hundred feet into the hillside attempting to contact what he hoped was a deeply buried ore body. Ever the optimist, he claimed at various times to have struck gold, silver, or cinnabar, whichever was most in demand at the time. Probably not much came from it. Exploration is hazardous and not recommended. At mile 2 the trail becomes rough and rocky, appearing bleached and iron stained. Chemical weathering through hydrothermal activity is the cause.

At 2¼ miles is a jeep trail junction. The southern portion appears on old USGS maps, but the northern part was cut illegally by landowners in 1992. In this area in fall or early spring you might see much sought chanterelle mushrooms. The variety of wildflowers continues with checker lily, hound's tongue, mule ears and nightshade.

As the road surface becomes smooth at 2⅜ miles, the first of two scenic and steep grassy slopes appear. After the second field, an old erosion gully, enlarged dramatically by the March 1995 flood, has taken out part of the trail. Beyond, a hillside seep sports seepspring monkeyflower, yellow petals enclosing a red heart. It will flower into the summer with enough water.

No benches are found along the trail, but at mile 3 is a rock outcrop that has a perfect sitting dish. Here is a good picnic/rest site as you look way down into fir-shrouded Simmons Canyon. In this area, look for the first of many wagon wheel ruts. As you turn the corner, the Palisades burst into view. Vegetation changes from woodland and brush to open grasslands with few trees and lots of chaparral. This reflects a change in the type of volcanic rock. These lapilli tuff units are much coarser and indicate your approach to an eruptive center.

At 3⅜ miles you come to the distinctive and well-named Bald Hill. Geologically it is an andesite intrusive that has forced its way up through older rock. Along the base is an old dugout spring that once served as a watering hole for horses hauling freight wagons. If you feel energetic a detour to the crest of Bald Hill (state park property) is rewarded by one of the best views in the county. All of Napa Valley is visible from Calistoga to Napa, and to the north the entire stretch of the Palisades to Mount St. Helena.

Just past Bald Hill is a junction with a fire road, the route favored by jeepers in the four-wheel-drive days. Although in places a narrow corridor of buckbrush and ceanothus, the regular trail is much easier. The sweet lilac smell of white, yellow, and blue ceanothus flowers is for me the scent of California spring. After a stand of chamise, turn a corner for close-up views of Palisades outliers. On the road and cliffs are vitriophyres, chunks of black obsidian glass speckled white with feldspar crystals. They are encased in a matrix that once flowed as mud after torrential rains (geological term — lahar).

At mile 4 appear the best set of wagon wheel ruts on the trail, almost five inches at their deepest. The wooden

wheels of freight wagons were capped with steel for protection. After many trips, ruts were formed in the relatively soft rock. The fire road shortcut joins the trail at a saddle. A smooth stretch of trail suddenly turns dramatic as it swings around a narrow turn, bordered by steep cliffs on one side and, on the other side, a dropoff supported by stone buttressing built by Chinese labor. A rusting hulk of a vehicle lies half buried in brush, legacy of an unlucky driver.

For the next mile the trail is mostly solid rock, one reason a trip from the mines to Calistoga took all day. Mountain bikers will pay the price of their ambition on this stretch. Now the Palisades are directly in view. They are composed of volcanic mud flows, agglomerate and welded tuffs. It is here the volcanic eruptions were most violent. The Palisades are the upper layer of a series of step faults; the lower sets are seen at the base. Perched above are columnar andesite columns, much like the basalt columns at Devil's Postpile in the Sierra.

At 4⅞ miles you reach the trail's high point and official end, and enter the shade of oak/bay forest. At this unlikely but beautiful site, the Holm family homesteaded at the century's turn. A few apple trees are left in the orchard. On the left side of the trail are remnants of two stone houses and a barn. Directly up the hillside is a deep, round, fern-rimmed spring that was their water source.

PETRIFIED FOREST LOOP

The only petrified redwood forest in the world

DIRECTIONS: From Calistoga drive northwest on Highway 128, turn left on Petrified Forest Road. Drive 3.5 miles to the entrance on the right.

HOURS: 10–5 every day in winter, 10–6 in summer. Closed Christmas and New Years.

FEE: $3 per person

DISTANCE: ½ mile. Wheelchair access for at least half the loop.

GRADE: Easy. Minimal elevation gain and loss.

BEST TIME: All year

INFO: Petrified Forest, 707/942-6667

SUGGESTIONS: Recently a new trail about ½ mile long was constructed to a large ashfall area and more petrified trees, with a view of Mount St. Helena. There is a tour every Sunday at 2 p.m. or by appointment.

NOTE: Check out the enormous valley oak that stands in front of the gift shop. It is now well over 600 years old. From the size of this giant you can roughly calculate the ages of other large oaks.

Fifty million years ago the West Coast's climate was cooler and wetter, and redwood forests stretched from California to Alaska. Their range had shrunk by the time the Petrified Forest was buried three and a half million years ago. Researchers still debate the mechanics of its demise. Was it felled by a volcanic blast from the northeast, or did it fall on its own? If from a violent blast, different ash types suggest separate events rather than one.

Whatever the mechanism, the method of burial is clear. Thousands of years of eruptions buried the trees in rhyolitic volcanic ash. Silica, leached from the rhyolite by water, infiltrated the wood fibers as they decomposed, cell by cell. The trees slowly petrified, literally turned to stone (petrifaction is from Latin, "turning to stone").

Gradual uplift of this site, combined with erosive weathering agents, had partially exposed some trees when they were discovered in the 1850s. They were left undisturbed for twenty years. Then a Swedish sailor, weary of the sea, settled here in 1871 to raise cows. After uncovering the redwoods while clearing his field, he quickly saw their value as a tourist attraction.

Charlie Evans, known as Petrified Charlie, played host to Scottish author Robert Louis Stevenson in June1880. Stevenson, writing in *The Silverado Squatters*, was more interested in the Swede than the ancient trees:

> And the forest itself? Well, on a tangled, briery hillside — for the pasture would bear a little further cleaning up, to my eyes — there lie scattered thickly various lengths of petrified trunk, such as the one already mentioned. It is very curious, of course, and ancient enough, if that were all. Doubtless, the heart of the geologist beats quicker at the sight; but for my part, I was mightily unmoved. Sight-seeing is the art of disappointment.

Evans sold the Forest following Stevenson's visit, and ownership then changed hands several times. Around 1910 it was bought by Frenchwoman Ollie Bockee (pronounced

Bokay). She immediately began excavations of several partially buried trees, including the tunnel to unearth the Monarch. She built the ranchhouse in 1915, and popularity of the site soared. Aunt Ollie died in 1951, but ownership is retained by her heirs.

In 1978 the Forest was declared California Historical Landmark number 915. Since 1988 there has been continuous upgrading, including new excavations and a new trail. The Petrified Forest has upwards of 75,000 visitors a year, at least a quarter of whom are from foreign countries.

TRAIL NOTES:

As you pass through the turnstile, look for a wooden arrow at the trailhead. There is a large chunk of petrified wood that you can touch and examine closely. Most of the ½-mile walk will be through a mix of evergreen forest (Douglas fir, madrone, live oak, gray pine), and chaparral species like toyon and manzanita. Ahead of you lie nine petrified tree sites.

The first site you come to is the Pit Tree, the only petrified pine tree among its stone redwood neighbors. In winter it may be partially submerged in water. This was part of the petrifaction process and does no harm. Employees sometimes use a high-power water spray to remove moss from trees without damaging the trunks.

Nearby is the Gully Tree. Long after burial and petrifaction, it broke into fragments through stress of gradual earth movement. The trail veers right and vegetation turns xerophytic briefly (scrub oak and chamise).

Just beyond a grassy meadow before ¼ mile is a collection called the Petrified Woodpile. A bench is provided where one can contemplate a lifelike Lilliputian-scale model of a miner and his donkey underneath a pure stand of mature manzanita.

As the loop veers right again The Giant and The Queen lie close together. Each has its own viewing platform. The Queen is especially impressive. As if denying her own death and petrifaction, she has generated from her stone body a live tree. (Later on, note the 1911 photograph of The Queen in the gift shop. An auto is parked next to it. The young oak is noticeably smaller).

Halfway through your

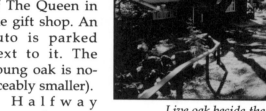
Live oak beside the old ranchhouse

walk is the Monarch or Tunnel Tree, the largest in the Forest at 105 feet. Instead of removing an entire hillside, the tree has sensibly been excavated by tunnel. The public was once allowed inside but today, liability prohibits entry. A longtime employee informed me it is constantly caving in. On the plus side, the tree is actually better seen today due to improved lighting and removal of a fence.

The last tree on the loop is the Robert Louis Stevenson Tree. This is the one the Scottish author was so unimpressed with when shown by owner, Petrified Charley Evans. The trail begins its descent. You'll pass a bronze relief plaque of Charley Evans with his pipe and Robert Louis Stevenson. Descend through magnificent old live oaks to the ranchhouse.

The Bockee ranchhouse has a fine, rustic, old-fashioned character about it. The pace is slower here and eases one back in time. Exit through the museum/gift shop. Both are well worth browsing. The geological display by Sonoma State professor Terry Wright is excellent. Pull up a chair at the 'library' and read Elise Mattison's short article "California's Fossil Forest." Or browse through the visitor registers that go back to the 1940s. Some people have found friends' and relatives' entries from years back.

BOTHE-NAPA VALLEY STATE PARK

Napa Valley's most popular state park

DIRECTIONS: The park is halfway between Saint Helena and Calistoga on Highway 29.

FEE: $5 day use

BEST TIME: Spring, summer

INFO: Bothe-Napa Valley State Park, 707/942-4575

SUGGESTIONS: Bicyclists may use Lower Ritchey Canyon Trail, and Spring Trail to the turnaround. Horseback riders can take advantage of a concession begun in 1995. A native plant garden used by the Wappo people is located next to the visitor's center.

TRAILHEAD: At Horse Trailer parking lot, a short distance beyond the campground turnoff on the right-hand side. All trails begin here except the History Trail, which you will find by continuing to the end of the paved road paralleling the highway.

So much began here, so many pioneers are connected with Bothe Park, that it is like a history of the Napa Valley itself. Some highlights follow.

The Wappo people, closely related to the Coast Yuki of the

northern Mendocino coast, occupied Napa Valley for at least four thousand years. They were composed of three tribelets, the northern Mishewal (Warrior People), the central Mutistul (North Valley), and the southern Meyahk'mah (Water Going Out Place). Each tribelet had mountain, valley and stream in their territory. Although they respected these boundaries, they practiced guardianship of the land rather than ownership.

The area we know as Bothe Park was home to the Mutistul Wappo, who had an encampment near Ritchey Creek known as Kaliholmanok. They would live here at various times throughout the year depending on factors like the weather and where the best food sources were to be found. The Wappo used and respected the full variety of the plant world, gathering plants for food, ceremony, technology (like basket making) and medicine.

Acorns, the staff of life, were gathered from the black oak and tanbark oak in fall to be made into soup, mush and bread. Bulbs of wild onion, brodiaea and mariposa lily, known as Indian potatoes, were cooked or eaten raw. Shellfish and salmon, from the Napa River, and abundant game rounded out their diet. Blue elderberry was cut into splitstick rattles for ceremonial dance. Sedge and redbud were highly prized for their strength and flexibility in basket making. The Wappo made baskets, a difficult skill to master, of all sizes and uses, including tight-weave baskets that were totally waterproof. Yerba santa and angelica were used for many ailments, as well as sandbar willow whose bark provided a kind of aspirin.

Traveling ancient trails, the Wappo people made an annual trek to Bodega Bay to trade with Coast Miwok for jewelry and clamshell bead currency. They also gathered and dried seaweed and salt to supplement their diet.

The thread of life the Wappo wove for millennia was unraveled in twenty short years, from 1836 to 1856. The Mexican government waged war on the Wappo and white man's diseases weakened the tribe. Most devastating was the taking of Wappo land by the settlers, putting the natives out of house and home. Some fled to the refuge of Li'leek near Clear Lake. Some blended into the culture. Between 1851 and 1856 the remaining 500 Wappo were bound and driven by United States troops to locations far from their ancestral lands.

Dr. Edward T. Bale, who some say survived a shipwreck on the Monterey coast, married into the Vallejo family in 1839. General Mariano Vallejo, commander at the Sonoma mission, granted Bale nearly 18,000 acres from Rutherford to Calistoga in 1841. Showing his sense of humor he named it *Rancho Carne Humana* (meaning human flesh), a play on the early name Callojomanas. The controversial Bale was once publicly flogged by General Vallejo's brother, Salvador Vallejo, for alleged slander. Later Bale was convicted of attempted murder of Salvador but released for political reasons. Despite his faults, which included excessive drinking, he was a hard worker and made a shrewd business decision to build a grist mill (see page 46, "Bale's Grist Mill").

The golden age of settlement by American overland pioneers lasted nearly thirty years from 1841 to the coming of the railroad. Two of these pioneers who came to Napa Valley were Reason Tucker and Florentine Kellogg. Tucker and Kellogg made their way over the Great American Desert and into California in 1846. They missed being caught by the same Sierra snows that trapped the Donner party by only twenty-four hours. When Tucker heard of the Donners' plight, he made four trips to rescue the survivors. He settled on a choice farm site on Ritchey Creek near present day Bothe Park. Some of his descendents still live in this area. In exchange for iron work on the Bale Mill, Florentine Kellogg received land on the south side of Mill Creek and built the oldest surviving frame house in Napa Valley, now owned by the Lyman family.

Historical firsts are plentiful here. In 1847 Sarah Graves Fosdick, widowed and orphaned by the Donner Party ordeal, opened the first American school in Napa Valley in a buckeye grove just across the road from the Bale Mill. At first it was a mere shelter of branches that allowed rain to pour in. This site is now part of Bothe-Napa Valley State Park.

The White Church was also a first in Napa Valley, built in 1853 and named for preacher Asa White. The crude structure had separate seating arrangements for men and women. Tramps burned it down around the turn of the century. A plaque marks the spot in the woods near the park's picnic area. A stone's throw away is the Pioneer Cemetery, first one in Napa Valley. Many of the Tucker family are buried here.

Both Reason Tucker and Florentine Kellogg would have

Bale's Grist Mill

Wheat replaced hide tanning as the number one industry in Napa County during the gold rush and continued to be important until 1890. Edward Bale employed pioneers Ralph Kilburn and Florentine Kellogg who built the mill by 1846. John Conn made the first millstones from material he found in the canyon behind the mill. The twenty-foot overshot wheel was powered by Mill Creek water brought in flumes originally made of dugout redwood logs. In the meantime the mercurial Dr. Bale got bitten by the gold fever and went to the Sierra foothills to prospect. By 1849 he had contracted, some say, a real fever and died that year in his adobe home off present Whitehall Lane. He left the mill and adjoining land to his daughter Isadora.

By 1853 Napa County was second only to Santa Clara County for wheat production in California. In fact, the only two grist mills north of San Mateo were the Bale Mill, and Chiles Mill in Chiles Valley. The original twenty-foot waterwheel was replaced by the present thirty-six-foot overshot wheel (meaning water sluices off the top), the largest been content to spend their old age in Napa Valley. Tucker and Kellogg had land holdings around the valley and Kellogg was active in local politics. But a claim to Tucker's land by Edward Bale's daughter, Isadora Bruck, went to the California Supreme Court. A contract with the previous owner was declared invalid, and Tucker lost everything in 1872. He moved to Santa Barbara to make a new life, as did Florentine Kellogg who was embittered by all the costly lawsuits against his friends and neighbors. Reason Tucker's son, George, married to Kellogg's daughter, remained in the valley. Their house is now used as headquarters for the state park. Tucker Farm Center and Tucker Road near the park recall the role played by the Tucker family in Napa Valley.

By the early 1870s two San Francisco families who

historic wooden wheel of its kind in the United States. Isadora Bale, now Mrs. Louis Bruck, built the Mill Pond in 1859 to ensure a steady supply of water for the mill. They sold Bale Mill the next year. Through the 1870s the Grist Mill (now the property of W.W. Lyman) was a successful business, and the granary served for dances, meetings and other social events. The wheat industry declined in the 1880s, but the Bale Mill continued intermittently as a custom milling operation until 1905 when it closed permanently.

W.W. Lyman continued the upkeep of the mill until his death in 1921. His widow, Sarah, sold it to the Native Sons of the Golden West soon after. The mill became a California State Historic Landmark in 1939 and two years later it was deeded to the county of Napa. In 1972 it was on the National Register of Historic Places, and incorporated into the state park system in 1974. After a long restoration it was reopened in 1983. When the waterwheel, flume and gearing were restored in 1988, the wheel began turning again for the first time in 109 years. You can watch the milling operations most summer weekends and purchase genuine stone-ground flour.

bought country estates here ultimately were instrumental in the formation of the park. W.W. Lyman began to acquire property in 1871, buying the Grist Mill and thirty acres for $10,000, mainly to protect water rights. Ultimately he owned 1,000 acres in this area. He moved into the house built by F.E. Kellogg in 1849 which is essentially unchanged today.

Dr. Hitchcock bought property in Ritchey Canyon in 1872, later building a summer home he called Lonely. Dr. Hitchcock is better known for his eccentric daughter nicknamed Firebelle Lillie. Besides chasing fire engines in San Francisco, one of her famous stunts was riding the train from Vallejo to Bale Station on the cowcatcher. The Hitchcocks planted orchard and vineyard on the hillsides and logged some trees. Most of the redwoods though, had been cut by earlier pioneers. Drag lines used to haul the trees out by oxen later became hiking trails.

After Lillie Hitchcock Coit died in 1929, Reinhold Bothe

The Hitchcock Barn, c. late 19th century

bought 1,000 acres and developed his "Paradise Park." It eventually had forty-one cabins, eighty-six tent cabins, tennis and bocce ball courts, stables and a lodge. The swimming pool was built in 1941, still used today as an unusual feature of a state park. One casualty of that era was Lonely, burned in 1938. Reinhold Bothe's mother, the resident, was forced to jump from the flaming structure.

After several attempts to sell over the years, Bothe sold his place to State Parks and Recreation in 1960. The lodge was removed, but some cabins are used by park staff today. The swimming pool remains a popular summer attraction. In 1981, campers, once forced to endure the sound of large trucks all night, were treated to a new remote campground with fifty sites, ten of the walk-in variety.

Today Bothe-Napa Valley State Park has 8½ miles of trails for hikers through one of the easternmost stands of redwoods in California. The rare and endangered Clara Hunt's milkvetch (*Astragalus clarianus*) is found in the park. Mountain lion, bobcat and rare bear sightings contribute to the park's wild nature. It has eighty-four species of birds including six kinds of woodpeckers, perhaps as many as when this was Native American land.

HISTORY TRAIL

DISTANCE:	1 ⅛ miles one way
GRADE:	Moderate

TRAIL NOTES:

Soon after the trail begins, a large boulder with a plaque marks the site of the White Church, the first built in Napa Valley (1853). Before ⅛ mile a side trail leads to the Pioneer Cemetery, also the first in the valley. If you like old cemeteries, don't miss this. Many of the pioneer Tucker family and their descendents are buried here. In 1958 vandals knocked down the fence and headstones, but today the cemetery is restored, with a fresh coat of paint on the white picket fence.

A sign points to the middle path at a three-way junction. The trail climbs steeply, flanked by young mixed forest of madrone, black oak, Douglas fir and tan oak. By contrast, down in the draw are magisterial old growth Douglas firs. The trail levels at ¼ mile then climbs gradually. Very young trees seem to indicate orchard or vineyard once occupied this slope.

Soon you reach the high point. It's all level or downhill from here. Glimpses of hillside vineyard on Spring Mountain are seen to the west at ½ mile. Smooth claret-colored trunks of manzanita have grown into twenty- and thirty-foot trees. The best views to the west are before ¾ mile.

The trail descends to a crossing of a small tributary of Mill Creek. Watch for poison oak close to the trail. The terrain opens to oak and grassland at mile 1 and soon a side trail leads to Mill Pond. The stone dam was built in 1859 by Isadora Bruck, daughter of Edward Bale, and her husband, to store water to power the large Grist Mill wheel. You make a second bridge crossing and suddenly huge valley oaks appear draped with Spanish moss. Not even the buckeyes escape this beard-like epiphyte, a lichen sometimes called tree net.

The trail ends at 1⅛ miles at the historic Grist Mill (a visit is highly recommended). Across the creek from the Mill is the Lyman House, the oldest frame house in the valley. It was built from lumber cut in this canyon by Florentine Kellogg at the time of the gold rush. A large bridge across Mill Creek (always lush with redwood, spice bush and alder) leads to the parking lot.

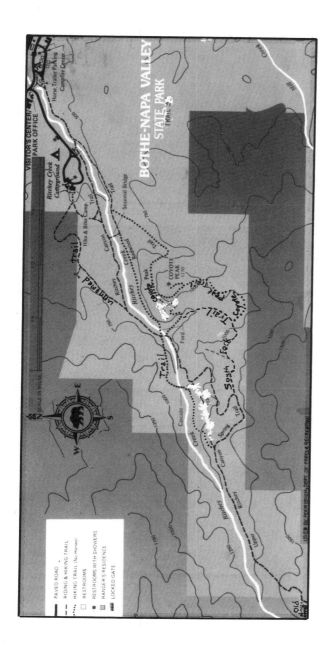

BOTHE-NAPA VALLEY STATE PARK

PAVED ROAD
RIDING & HIKING TRAIL
HIKING TRAIL (No Horses)
RESTROOMS
RESTROOMS WITH SHOWERS
RANGER'S RESIDENCE
LOCKED GATE

RITCHEY CANYON TRAIL AND UPPER RITCHEY CANYON TRAIL

The longest hike in the park takes you to an old homestead.

DISTANCE: 4⅛ miles one way
GRADE: Moderate

TRAIL NOTES:

Starting at Horse Trailer Parking, the trail parallels the access road, then crosses a paved service road. The trail is shaded by buckeye, maple, Douglas fir, madrone and black oak. Veer left at Ritchey Creek and join the gravel road at ¼ mile. Soon come to the first of two drinking fountains. The forest is now mainly redwood and fir, with thickets of spice bush more than ten feet tall beside Ritchey Creek.

After ½ mile is the Redwood Trail junction. Stay right at the sign. At the time of my hike, the "R" in "Ritchey Canyon" was gone, perhaps removed by someone impressed with the poison oak here. Pass the campground on your right with the creek now on your left side. This stream is popular with kids in the summer who go wading and searching for crawdads. Related to lobsters, these crayfish are interesting creatures — they have eyes on movable stalks and can regrow their pincer hands.

At ⅞ mile is Lonely, once the summer home of the Hitchcock family. The Hitchcock house burned in 1938. In the 1940s the existing house was built and used as a gambling hall without the Bothe's permission. The stone fountain dates from the Hitchcock days as well as the large redwood barn just uptrail. A nearby drinking fountain is the last guaranteed potable water. A side road to the right leads to the campground.

A short spur, at mile 1, goes left across Ritchey Creek to Redwood Trail, formerly spanned by the now discarded bridge. Riparian vegetation like blackberry, elk clover, thimbleberry and wild grape grow jungle-like in or near the creek. Several volunteer trails lead to more open sites by the creek, sometimes to small redwood groves thick with redwood duff underfoot. The pileated woodpecker is often seen or heard in this area, although he can be anywhere in the park.

Before 1¾ miles take the first trail junction to the right. To the left is Redwood Trail, and just beyond, Spring and South Fork trail junctions. Take Ritchey Canyon Trail and climb high above the creek then drop to meet it at almost 2 miles. Even on a hot day in a drought year, this site is cool. The water is cold and often a down-canyon breeze blows. There is a smooth rock in the stream on which to sit and cool your heels.

The trail climbs most steeply in the next ¼ mile, passing a spring-fed tributary of Ritchey Creek. Watch for dogwood flowering white in the spring and leaves turning pink in the fall. Trail surface around 2¼ miles is steep and loose. Above this section are two manzanitas up to twenty-five feet high and one foot in diameter. Scrub oak, toyon, bay and black oak reflect the drier slope.

A major trail junction at 2⅜ miles is unusual because of full sun exposure. You can see all of Upper Ritchey Canyon to the west. Beyond is Diamond Mountain (2,375 feet). Peak 2,085 sits above a steep volcanic cliff to the northwest. Turn right onto the Upper Ritchey Canyon Trail and soon dive back into the forest.

At a creek crossing with an old wooden bridge is a twin-trunked alder tree high enough to compete with the redwoods. Even summer-dry creek beds can have underground water to grow large specimens like this one. Most of the redwoods you see in the canyon are second growth. The original redwoods were cut 150 years ago as the best building wood available. Just before mile 3 a shady moist spot under redwoods holds a patch of wild ginger. They have dark green, heart-shaped leaves with an indentation at the stem. If you are hiking alone, this area is quiet and isolated enough to bring to mind a quote by W.W. Lyman Jr. from his memoirs: *"I used to like to go where the trees were tall and close together and the underworld seemed alive with mysterious intimations."*

The next tributary stream crossing is exceptionally wide for this canyon. Maple trees grow right in the creek bed. Around 3¼ miles you get a closer view of those volcanic cliffs on canyon's north side.

Watch for an unmarked junction at 3½ miles leading to the Traverso homestead. A small trail leads across a creek through horsetail and vinca. Some vandal has taken the plating from a stone plaque remembering Sam Vance, who liked this site. A meadow on the steep hillside has fig and apple trees. In the fall at least one of the apple trees has delicious fruit. This is a fine picnic site surrounded by redwood and fir. In the upper meadow coyote brush and pickeringia are slowly invading, but star thistle has already performed a hostile takeover.

Italians Biaggio and Margheritta Traverso built a home here in 1884. When the widow Margheritta filed for proof of homestead in 1890 she claimed the following improvements: a four room house, a barn, three cleared acres, one quarter mile of fencing, three quarters of an acre of grapes, and a few fruit trees for a total worth of 200 dollars. Later on, relatives of the chocolate family from San Francisco, Ghirardelli, bought this site.

To reach the trail's end, return to the unmarked junction and head uphill. The trail bends left and widens to a road, once the main access from Spring Mountain Road. Douglas fir, black oak, and tan oak predominate. You are allowed one view, as the forest thins, of Napa Valley and the Howell Mountains to the east. At 4⅛ miles a large yellow sign facing uphill marks the state park boundary. Just beyond is Ritchie Creek Vineyards. Return the way you came.

REDWOOD TRAIL

The easiest and most pleasant hike in the park

DISTANCE: 1 mile one way
GRADE: Easy

TRAIL NOTES:

The trail begins ½ mile up the Ritchey Canyon Trail. Veer left at the junction as the trail turns to a narrower dirt path. On the moist, north-facing slope sword ferns stay green into the droughty fall months. The periwinkle (*Vinca major*) that used to cover the stream banks has been removed leaving the flood plain more natural.

As the terrain opens and becomes drier, Oregon oak appears. Pass the Coyote Peak Trail junction before ⅜ mile. A spur to the Ritchey Canyon Trail crosses the creek at ½ mile. From here bikes and horses are off limits. A goose pen of redwoods has five young trees in a circle twelve feet across, the progeny of a giant cut 150 years ago.

After a brief uphill climb look for star Solomon's seal in the spring. Usually seen singly or in small groups, at this site it covers the ground en masse.

The trail climbs a narrow path beyond ¾ mile and traverses a steep, exposed hillside. There has been recent rerouting of the trail here and at the creek crossing at just before 1 mile. Ritchey Creek can be uncrossable in high water but usually it's an easy rock hop.

Redwood Trail ends at mile 1. Take Ritchey Canyon Trail back for a loop or continue on Coyote Peak or Spring Trails.

COYOTE PEAK TRAIL

An excellent and popular moderate loop hike

DISTANCE: 2¼ miles to peak or 5-mile loop
GRADE: Moderate
DIRECTIONS: Take Ritchey Canyon Trail and Redwood Trail just over ¾ mile to Coyote Peak trailhead.

TRAIL NOTES:

Soon after commencing Coyote Trail look for a rock wall on the left. Beyond it is an old hillside vineyard site, planted by the Hitchcock family, with a few original redwood stakes. The trail then rises steeply through some tan oak and dogwood. In the next ¼ mile are several dead Douglas firs pockmarked with woodpecker holes. The flat-headed borer is a beetle responsible for many dead firs in this park.

Redwoods are usually seen in shady river canyons, but here around ¾ mile on the hillside just below a ridgetop are redwoods. Look trailside for flowering wild iris in the spring. Before mile 1 come around the shoulder of Coyote Peak for a splendid view of Ritchey Canyon watershed. At 1⅛ miles is a trail junction. Go left 500 feet to the summit. On the way you pass young redwoods on the south-facing slope, again defying conventional wisdom.

Once in the 1980s I arrived on top and was swallowed by an opaque thicket of trees. There was no view, no sense of having arrived anywhere. The careful clearing of some trees and brush has made this a more satisfying destination. Now you can see vineyards on Spring Mountain to the west, and Schramsberg Vineyards and winery to the north, with Mount St. Helena beyond.

Return to the trail junction and turn left to make a loop hike. Follow a saddle, then, before sinking into Ritchey Creek watershed, you have a profile of Coyote Peak and Mount St. Helena on its left. Your descent is steep to a perennial creek just before 2 miles where springs nourish chain fern, thimbleberry, great thickets of spice bush and some of the finest redwoods in the park. Soon after is the South Fork Trail junction. Coyote Peak Trail ends here. Turn right and continue downhill on South Fork Trail to return via Ritchey Canyon, or turn left for more hiking.

ADDITIONAL TRAILS

SOUTH FORK TRAIL is 1⅜ miles long, starting near the four-way junction and ending on Spring Trail. At ¾ mile is a junction with Coyote Peak Trail and at about 1 mile it crosses a ridge between watersheds. At this point a short trail takes you to a view of the upper Napa Valley.

SPRING TRAIL is a ¾ mile continuation of the Ritchey Canyon Trail. At the four-way junction, cross Ritchey Creek and go steeply up the wide road past the South Fork junction and the springs that supply the park. The road ends in a circle turnaround where a narrower trail continues to the junction with Upper Ritchey Canyon Trail.

An **UNNAMED TRAIL**, ¾ mile long, starts at the back of the campground near walk-in site #31. The trail begins on a wide gravelled path, then veers right onto a dirt road after 200 feet. Around ¼ mile the trail/road continues as an easement through private property. After reentering the park, take the middle fork at the ½-mile junction and descend through chaparral, then forest to meet Ritchey Canyon Trail.

CEDAR ROUGHS

The largest stand of Sargent cypress in the world

DIRECTIONS: From just north of Saint Helena, take Deer Park Road to Angwin. Deer Park continues as North Howell Mountain Road into Pope Valley. Turn right on Chiles and Pope Valley Road, then left on Pope Canyon Road. After you pass the old gravel pit, look for a long guard rail on the right. Park at the end of the guard rail. Lake Berryessa is about 3 miles east from here. Look for a large tree marked with orange tape across the creek. The trail starts near there.

DISTANCE: ⅞ mile one way

GRADE: Moderate

ELEVATION GAIN: 500 feet

BEST TIME: Late winter, spring

INFO: Bureau of Land Management, 707/468-4000

WARNING: Heavy rains in winter make Pope Creek impassable.

Cedar Roughs has had little historical use. The rugged nature of this country and the dense cover of cypress have discouraged both man and beast. Tentative mining explorations for mercury, magnesium, and chromite showed these deposits too poor for commer-

*cial venture. Now under the Bureau of Land Management, plans
are to keep its wild nature essentially unchanged.*

In the fall of 1871 J.J. Walters discovered three mineral
springs off Pope Canyon Road. They were surrounded on
the west, east, and north by steep hills, with a view south to
what was then called Cedar Mountain. With partner J.W.
Smittle, Walters made improvements to encourage summer
visitors. The mineral waters were said to cure ailments like
rheumatism, asthma and dyspepsia, and to ease heart
disease. Daily stagecoaches brought the firm and the infirm
alike from Rutherford. Board and lodging at the hotel was
only $8 a week. Mineral drinking water was bottled and
shipped from here by 1886.

Near the mouth of Trout Creek, where it empties into
Pope Creek, Elisha Cornelius Samuels discovered his own
springs in 1881. Samuels Springs was bought by G.R. Morris
ten years later and became a first-class resort. In front of the
large hotel, an enormous fountain served as the centerpiece
for the resort. There was room for 150 people in cottages
and tents. Morris provided a grass tennis court, croquet
grounds and a dance hall for his guests' entertainment, while
a dairy, a vegetable garden and a fifteen-ton capacity ice
house provided for their needs. By 1901 daily mail and
newspapers were delivered from Saint Helena. There was
even a resident physician.

After World War I, these two establishments began a
long, slow and genial decline. Samuels Springs was run as
a rehabilitation camp for kids in the 1950s. After it was abandoned, Napan Bob McKenzie remembers the extensive van-
dalism he saw there on a visit in 1957. The damage included
two pianos smashed to pieces, one a beautiful upright rose-
wood grand piano.

Walters Springs fared little better. It was operated into
the 1950s, run by a character named Mabel Wise. Vandals
sacked most of the cottages after it closed, despite the fact
that Mabel still lived on the property. Regulars returned

every summer for another twenty-five years after its closure. In a 1981 interview, Mabel told how the mineral waters once cured her of a rattlesnake bite. Living alone so many years, she learned to be resourceful and fearless. One night, hearing a clatter outside, she looked out her window to see a bear looting her trash cans only inches away. She leaned over and kissed him!

A Marin architect in the early 1980s proposed to resurrect Walters Springs as a modern health spa. Plans came to naught.

In 1980 Cedar Roughs was declared a Wilderness Study Area by the Bureau of Land Management. Three years later it was designated an Area Of Critical Environmental Concern and a Research Natural Area (ACEC-RNA). A final Environmental Impact Statement in 1986 recommended Cedar Roughs as unsuitable for wilderness designation.

Presently the only trail in the area ends more than a mile from the ACEC-RNA. There is no legal access to the heart of Cedar Roughs yet but exciting plans are in the works. Government agencies are currently working on buying key parcels. One day BLM will build a trail along the central ridge of Cedar Roughs (west of Trout Creek Ridge). It will connect two trailheads, one at the existing Pope Creek trailhead, the other across from the Bureau of Reclamation headquarters at Lake Berryessa. There will be no improve-

Cedar or cypress?

Five-thousand-six-hundred-acre Cedar Roughs should really be called Cypress Roughs. It contains the largest, genetically pure stand of Sargent cypress in the world. It is uniquely suited to the serpentine soil, but dry conditions in the upper elevations stunt these trees to ten feet creating a weird pygmy forest. Cedar Roughs is also unique for being the only known bear breeding area in Napa County. There is a small but stable population of about ten black bear.

ments other than the trail and improved parking at the Pope Canyon trailhead.

TRAIL NOTES:

Once past the indistinct start of the trail, you'll find it in fair shape despite its unmaintained status. This east-facing hillside supports a wide mix of plants like gray pine, toyon, buckeye, scrub oak, bay, and in spring, wildflowers like Indian warrior and shooting star. Cross a seasonal stream bed beyond ⅛ mile and enter one of the largest scrub oak for-

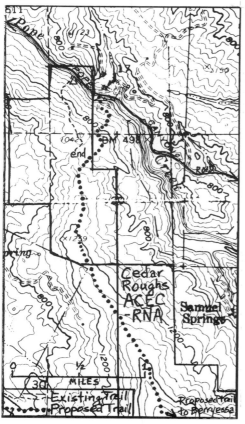

ests around, up to twenty feet high.

Watch for poison oak at ¼ mile as the trail climbs steeply past a single old manzanita. You'll go through some ceanothus (wild lilac) then a brushier section as the trail turns rocky like a creek bed. The southeast-trending trail now turns due east on the first of several switchbacks.

At ⅝ mile look northeast past ranch buildings to the horizon. Berryessa Peak (3,057 feet) can be seen with its relay station towers and fire lookout. Vegetation thins at ¾ mile as you approach the ridge. The trail levels off and a portion of Lake Berryessa becomes visible to the east. Soon you reach the ridgetop. In the valley immediately west is Saint Supery Vineyards off Dollarhide Road. To the south, Trout Creek Ridge, like a giant whale back, climbs and climbs to its apex at Iron Mountain (2,287 feet).

Walk along the ridgetop going east, then cross over to the west side. Along the trail are yerba santa and in spring, star zygadene, each of the six-petaled creamy-white flowers having a yellow gland at its base. Burn scars show in the regenerating chaparral. From the top of a knoll you will see another lower knoll, with scattered oaks. Between these knolls is a grassy swale. The trail fizzles out in this area around ⅞ mile. Return the same way.

Pope Creek below
Cedar Roughs

LAKE HENNESSEY

Superb waterfowl viewing in winter

DIRECTIONS: From Saint Helena drive east on Pope Street to Silverado Trail. Cross the Trail catercorner onto Howell Mountain Road. When Howell Mountain veers left, go straight on Conn Valley Road to the northwest corner of the lake. Skirt the lake until stopped by a locked metal gate. Park in one of the turnouts.

HOURS: One hour before sunrise until sunset.

DISTANCE: 2 miles one way

GRADE: Easy. Minimal elevation gain or loss.

BEST TIME: Winter, early spring

SUGGESTIONS: The picnic area at the base of the dam, off Highway 128, is open on weekends from Memorial Day to Labor Day. It has shade trees, tables, restrooms, water and a ballfield.

Irishman John Conn came to California in 1844 by way of Illinois. During construction of the Bale Mill in 1846 he took rock from a nearby hill and fashioned the first millstones. His claim to 6,000 acres of valley and mountain land east of Saint Helena was never formally granted by the Mexican government. He lost his land in the valley named for him

High water winter

and died in Napa, by one account, due to excessive drinking. His nephew, Connolly Conn, settled in Conn Valley in 1855.

In the mid-1880s work was begun to connect Rutherford and Monticello (in Berryessa Valley) via railroad. According to authors of a *Saint Helena Star* news article, the San Francisco and Clear Lake Railroad had cleared right-of-way on lower Sage Canyon skirting Conn Valley, then through steep upper Sage Canyon to Chiles Valley Road. By 1887 all work had been abandoned, with equipment like wheel barrows scattered where thrown.

The pastoral simplicity of Conn Valley remained unthreatened until World War II made Napa a commuter town for Mare Island Naval Base. Milliken Dam no longer supplied enough water for Napa's growing population, so the city bought 2,600 acres in Conn Valley in 1942. Conn Valley had several farms of apple orchards and grazing land. It's reported that the soil was not rich and was cultivated sparsely.

Work on the earthen dam began in 1945 after a summer of clearing the land of trees and farm buildings. It took only six months, using impacted water-impervious clay materials and rocks of all sizes, to build the dam 110 feet high and 200 feet thick at the base. It holds back 33,000 acre-feet of water from Conn, Chiles, Sage and Moore Creeks, sixteen times the capacity of its predecessor, Milliken Dam. Edwin R. Hennessey coordinated the city of Napa's water development for many years. The city council named the lake for him in 1951.

Engineers discovered a design flaw in 1963 when a wet winter caused the spillway to overflow and undercut Highway 128, closing the road. A concrete plug called an Australian Baffle was installed to divert the flow. Since then it has been a popular spectacle for locals to watch. During lake overflow, tons of water come churning down the channel at freeway speed, crash into the baffle with deafening booms, and create a geyser dozens of feet high. In the 1986 flood, fallout drift spray from the geyser was so heavy that drivers drove blind for a short section as windshield wipers slapped uselessly.

Fishing, boating and wildlife viewing are popular today with a new boat launch facility installed in 1990. The picnic site at the base of the dam is open weekends from Memorial Day to Labor Day.

In the winter Lake Hennessey is one of the best places in Napa County for viewing birds, especially waterfowl. A short list of birds one might see in a few hours would include: mourning dove, bluejay, red-winged blackbird, yellow warbler, meadowlark, junco, flicker, red-headed woodpecker, starling, seagull, crow, turkey vulture, kestrel, kingfisher, red-tailed hawk, Cooper's hawk, northern harrier, blue heron, mallard, coot, Canadian goose, pelican, cormorant, bald eagle, golden eagle and osprey.

TRAIL NOTES:

Take the right fork past the metal gate (left goes into private property) over a small creek to a sign making sure you know Lake Hennessey is the water supply for the city of Napa. Swimming or any acts of pollution are forbidden. Another fork in the road appears. Take the right one past another locked gate. Depending on the season, the lake may be right below the road or hundreds of feet away.

A mature gray pine forest stands on the left before ¼ mile. It is no coincidence that road cuts below it show grey-green shiny rock known as serpentine. Magnesium-rich serpentine soil is toxic to most trees, but gray pines love it. The day I went through, piles of pine cones lay below the trees, stripped clean of their tasty nuts by gray squirrels.

Lakeside, a tree stump is a favorite perch of the great blue heron. They are graceful flyers, holding their heads in close to form a U or S shape in the neck, while flapping wings evenly. Tall reeds nearby are great habitat for smaller birds.

Pass under oaks draped with Spanish moss at ¼ mile.

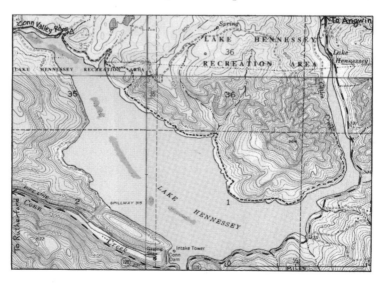

Top a small hill and as the road heads downhill, hillside vineyards on Pritchard Hill come into view to the southeast. The hills across Lake Hennessey are clothed in oak woodland or dense, mixed evergreen forest, while more exposed nearby slopes have chaparral or blue oak/gray pine. In the spring, masses of Ithuriel's spear and soap plant bloom among the grasses.

Just before ½ mile the road levels out and terrain is flat and open for the next ⅓ mile. This is a likely place to see the kestrel (sparrow hawk). The small, colorful falcon can be seen hovering over fields in search of prey. Sounds may carry far on a calm day. Conversations of fishermen far out on the lake can sometimes be heard word for word.

Across the lake at ¾ mile you can see the spillway, and to its left the intake tower and the earthen dam itself. The road begins a big swing to the left to circle an inlet bay. This is a favorite place for waterfowl to congregate. Large numbers of Canadian geese, coots, mallards and other ducks gather here.

A small, flat boulder on the left makes a fine resting bench at ⅞ mile. After one of the larger creek crossings at 1 mile, the vegetation changes dramatically. A small grove of Spanish moss-draped blue oaks seems like a tropical island compared to the flat, open terrain on either side. Drop down and to the left off the hill, passing under one of the larger blue oaks and into the open.

Before reaching the next tributary at 1½ miles, look northeast to a fine hillside of oak crowned with gray pines. In a wet winter, you may be lucky enough to spot a bald eagle or two perched in one of these pines. If you have never seen one, his great white head is unmistakable.

On a clear day, look to the northwest past Angwin where only the tops of the north, south and middle peaks of Mount St. Helena will be visible. Spring Mountain west of Saint Helena is also visible through a gap. The trail skirts the hillside past the creek, and as you turn left (east) traffic on Highway 128 will become noticeable.

At 1¾ miles the trail orientation turns once again to the north, and passes two aluminum shacks. These are unsigned outhouses. The road rises higher above the lake passing under live oaks. A gray pine arches way over the trail, distance horizontally from base to branch tips is fifty feet! Its trunk is riddled with acorn woodpecker holes, some stuffed with acorns. Woodpeckers have not stopped there, but dittoed a couple of nearby fence posts with holes too. The road now dips and twists through superb oak woodland.

The new boat launch facility comes into view across the lake. The road then dives and climbs to a gorgeous live oak-studded hilltop. To the southeast is a close view of Pritchard Hill and Chapellet Vineyards. At mile 2 you come to a locked gate and trail's end. A social trail leads downhill past some fruit trees, often an indicator of old homesteads. It ends in about ¼ mile. Return the same way.

NAPA VALLEY ECOLOGICAL RESERVE

The last significant stand of valley oaks in Napa Valley

DIRECTIONS: From Highway 29 at Yountville, go east on Madison for two blocks. Turn left on Yount, then right on Yountville Cross Road. After 1.1 miles, turn north into a small parking lot, just west of the new bridge.

From Silverado Trail the turnoff is slightly less than a mile.

DISTANCE: 1¼-mile loop

GRADE: Easy. Minimal elevation gain or loss.

BEST TIME: Spring and fall

WARNING: From December to April the footbridge may be inundated, preventing entry to eastern portion of the Reserve.

INFO: Dept. of Fish and Game, 707/944-5500

In 1836 this property formed part of the southern boundary of George Yount's *Rancho Caymus*. Low-lying areas at the confluence of Conn Creek and Napa River would flood during many wet winters, often to a depth of three or four feet. By the turn of the century a levee was built on the west bank of Napa River to keep all but the highest floods out.

In 1851 began a tradition of church revivals lasting 28 years. They took place in the flat grassy area just beyond the present parking lot, known as the Yountville Camp Grounds. The Disciples of Christ denominational church, also known as Campbellites, held meetings here annually. Headed by local pastor Stormy John McCorkle, they were enormously popular affairs lasting a week or two, with as many as 4,000 people coming from all over the state. Some participants brought their own camping equipment, but those without had special accommodations built for them. Cooking facilities and long tables were set up, to serve upwards of 1,000 meals a day. With the establishment of laundries, barber shops, a restaurant, and stores selling ice cream, candy, tobacco and cigars, the Yountville Camp Grounds each year became a temporary small city.

The Methodist-Episcopal church and the Seventh Day Adventists also used this site. The tradition of outdoor camp meetings gave way after 1879 to indoor city conventions. Use of the Yountville Camp Grounds after that was limited to cattle grazing. It is unlikely the ground was ever tilled for crops. The valley oak/bay laurel riparian forest on the eastern portion of the reserve is virtually unchanged since the days when George Yount first drove his cattle through the Napa River.

In 1974 threat of development prompted the Wildlife Conservation Board to buy this area to create the 73-acre Napa River Ecological Reserve. It was then turned over to California Department of Fish and Game for management. Farther up-valley, one hundred acres of valley floor oak woodland between Bale Lane and Ehlers Lane met a sadder fate. Over seventy-five oaks up to 400 years old were destroyed by Beaucannon winery for vineyard in 1989. This was one of the finest parts of Napa Valley.

The importance of the Napa Valley Ecological Reserve cannot be overstated. It is the last significant stand of valley oak riparian woodland left in Napa Valley. Walking through here for the first time in December 1994, I was stunned to discover this beautiful piece had survived. It has the only stretch of the Napa River I've seen that looks inviting enough to swim. In 1994 the Napa Solano Audubon was awarded a grant of $7,300 to improve the overgrown CCC trail, and install a descriptive sign, benches, public toilet and for the printing of bird, animal and plant lists and a trail guide. The new trail was built in June 1995. Other aspects of the plan are scheduled for completion by 1996.

TRAIL NOTES:

The trail heads north through the meadow once known as the Yountville Camp Grounds. Before the levee was built, the river plain may have been ½ mile wide here. Ascend to the levee top. Hundreds of sandbags were placed here during the floods of 1995, but could not prevent major damage to the levee. In June 1995 the levee was completely regraded and repaired.

As you head toward the river, vegetation on this old river terrace is dramatically different. The dominant overstory is valley and live oak with an understory of Santa Barbara sedge, Himalaya berry (wild blackberry), and common snowberry. As you drop down to the river, vegetation undergoes another quick transformation to willows, smartweed and sedge.

At river level, follow it upstream briefly, then cross a low wood and metal bridge to reach the east side. This bridge can be inundated from December to April. Just south, Conn Creek joins the Napa River. Ascending the bank, you come to a split in the trail just before ¼ mile. Either fork can be taken on this loop. We go left and come to a great meadow ringed by enormous valley oaks. One hundred fifty years ago much of Napa Valley looked like this.

The trail now leads you along the east bank of the Napa River, past wild plum, bay laurel, live oak and valley oaks overhead. Watch for poison oak among the sedge and snowberry. This area is comparable to the Nature Conservancy's Cosumnes River Preserve in Sacramento County. Steelhead trout are easily seen in the river shadows.

The trail veers right at ½ mile, passing a giant wild grape vine estimated at one hundred years old. The northern end of the trail is reached at ⅝ mile under a large wild plum. The trail begins to loop back, following the west bank of Conn Creek. The calls of acorn woodpecker, rufous-sided towhee, quail, and song sparrow will often be heard. Some of the rare and/or endangered plants to look for among the reserve's 238 species are Sebastopol meadowfoam, Gairdner's yampah, pink star tulip and camas.

The loop ends at 1⅛ miles where a side trail leads to Conn Creek. From here it is about ¼ mile back to the parking lot.

WEST BANK TRAIL

From the top of the levee turn left and continue along the river terrace. You'll notice that the same moral degenerates who vandalized the bridge have spray painted several oak trunks. After ¼ mile come to a postcard picture overview of the Napa River. When I visited in December 1994, a fallen oak limb spanned the riverbed. It was several feet in diameter and long as an average tree. After the flood in January there was no trace. You may return the same way or take any of several social trails down to the river for a loop.

ALSTON PARK

Napa City's second largest open space park

DIRECTIONS: From Highway 29 take Trower Avenue west. The southern park entrance is straight across Dry Creek Road. There is a second, north entrance .25 mile up Dry Creek Road.

DISTANCE: 2½-mile double loop

GRADE: Easy

BEST TIME: All year

INFO: Napa Parks and Recreation, 707/257-9529

Chipped mortars and obsidian flakes found in a 1991 survey suggest Native Americans occupied this site sometime in the past. In historical times, the land has sustained heavy livestock grazing. The park primarily consists of non-native grass hills with some native purple needle grass (*Stipa pulchra*). A recent California Native Plant Society survey recorded a diversity of plant life, suggesting the area is slowly recovering.

In 1971 seventy-one acres in the southern portion of today's park, known as the Thomas property, were for sale. It was mostly prune orchard then, with some pears, cherries, peaches and walnuts. In 1978 the City of Napa purchased all of the present Alston Park and had plans for a community center and recreation facilities. Two years later the city council approved baseball and softball diamonds and lighting, soccer fields, tennis courts, a pool, picnic tables, trails and a community hall. That's when, you might say, the prunes hit the orchard fan.

Disapproval of the idea erupted city wide. Wine growers were appalled that prime viticulture land would be paved over. Taxpayers refused to foot the maintenance bill. One group, the Citizens for Alston Alternatives, took out full page ads in the newspaper to ask pointed questions. Why sink $10 million into another recreation complex when neglected Kennedy Park was already there? The proposal was defeated in 1981.

Ten years later in 1991 Alston Park opened as a passive use open space park. It offers something for almost everyone — walkers, joggers, mountain bikers, equestrians and dog owners, who have formed their own support group — ADOG (Alston Dog Owners Group). The City of Napa owns it and Parks and Recreation maintains it. Users will find restrooms, water, and three picnic sites available in the 157-acre park. Eight well maintained trails provide three miles of walking. Trail maps are found at Napa Parks and Recreation, 1100 West Street near the Cine Dome Theatre in Napa.

TRAIL NOTES:
The following two loop trails allow you to see the entire park.

LOOP 1 (2 miles)
Take Valley View Trail to Orchard Trail past feral fruit trees. On the way are wooden bridges crossing two small creeks that flow in the winter. Past the north entrance continue on Dry Creek Trail. On the north side of the park is a major oak replanting project, young trees protected by plastic tubes. Stands of live oak, valley oak, and madrone on Dry Creek make excellent natural picnic sites in the spring.

From the west hilltop, in the forested slopes above

Redwood Creek, the henna-colored trunks of redwood stand out against the darker evergreens. Here, a dead-end side trail leads to the best part of the park. Don't miss it. It leads downhill past oaks draped with Spanish moss. In the flat below are valley oak and old buckeye trees, with wild grape in Redwood Creek, a cool place to head for in summer.

Back on Dry Creek Trail turn east and parallel an extensive vineyard that separates the north and south portions of the park. Just before joining the service road you pass the Pacifica Water Tank, built in 1960 in response to the exploding housing development in Brown's Valley. Join Valley View Trail. Immediately a connector trail leads to a picnic site and incipient Means (Memorial) Grove. Continue past two more trail junctions to Prune Picker Trail.

To the left is a giant wreck of a valley oak. One morning I saw a kestrel fly to the top of it with a meal. Chunks of fur

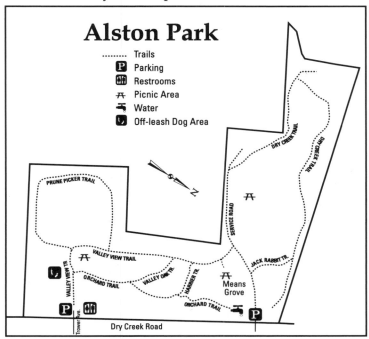

went flying every time he took a bite. The black-tipped red tail of the falcon was split, with the bottom half constantly bobbing up and down. Alston is a good place to see these beautiful raptors.

LOOP 2 (½ mile)

The Prune Picker Trail takes off from Valley View Trail and ends on the same trail, taking a loop around an abandoned orchard. It's a suitable length for a morning walk before work. It can be accessed also by a narrow entrance in the southeast corner of the park.

Along the Napa River Trail

WESTWOOD HILLS REGIONAL PARK

Oak woodland countryside within Napa city limits

DIRECTIONS: From Highway 29 in Napa take First Street exit west, then continue as it becomes Brown's Valley Road. After 1 mile the park entrance is on your left.

DISTANCE: 2-mile loop

GRADE: Easy

BEST TIME: All year

INFO: Napa Parks and Recreation, 707/257-9529

FACILITIES: Picnic tables, water fountain

SUGGESTIONS: Trail maps are available from the Carolyn Parr Nature Museum, found on the west border of the park. It's open weekends during the school year from 1–4 PM and during the summer Tuesday–Sunday 1–4. The museum has exhibits and dioramas depicting the plants, animals and geology of Napa County, plus children's and adult nature libraries.

Napa County Land Trust's Connally Ranch is at the corner of Brown's Valley Road and Thompson Avenue. Tours are by appointment only. For information call 707/252-3270.

Threat of housing development in the 1970s almost consigned Westwood Hills to history. In 1974 a developer proposed building 350 homes on this beautiful 110-acre parcel. The scaled-down version counter-offered by the city did not interest the developer. That's when the city proposed to buy the parcel for parkland.

For many years Westwood Hills was used for grazing cattle. When the old rancher died his heirs wished to sell. They liked the idea of saving the land as a park, and waited until sufficient money was appropriated. The City of Napa bought the land in 1975 for $160,000, about $1500 an acre. The man who spearheaded this effort was former Napa City Planner Mike Joell. The park opened in January 1976.

Literally thousands of hours of volunteer time went into building trails, installing benches and tables, and readying the park for opening. California Conservation Corps built many of the trails, the National Guard worked on some roads and today local environmental groups and the Boy Scouts still do maintenance and improvements.

Drought conditions in 1976 invited a grass fire to race through that first summer. Rocky Ridge Trail was created in a futile attempt to block the fire's progress. Eucalyptus on that ridge and in Gum Canyon were destroyed along with some live oaks. It was noticed that deer-browsed trees were saved while those with branches touching the ground caught fire.

New policies were set as a result. Because controlled burns were unsafe so close to urban areas, it was decided that 1) fuel sources like eucalyptus and Scotch broom should be eliminated, 2) all important trees should be kept trimmed above ground, 3) cattle would graze here May to October to moderate fuel sources, and 4) buffer zones around the park were necessary for public safety. Today, the persnickety eucalyptus cut to the ground after the fire have regrown, showing that element of the solution needs rethinking.

In 1980 the property just south of Hilltop was bought cheaply at auction by developer Leroy Young. Soon after, an exemption was granted to allow a water hookup. Despite vociferous public outcry, a large three-story house that includes a two-story racquet ball court was built. Still under construction, the house has never been occupied. After a neighbor filed a lawsuit, approximately 30 city code violations were discovered, including a lack of permits for transmission tower installation. A second exemption was sought for another house but denied. In the face of community opposition, individualist Young has shown his sense of humor by erecting a smiley face made of pvc pipe and lit by Christmas lights, visible at night all over the city.

Westwood Hills today enjoys great popularity throughout the year. There are no immediate plans for expansion, but one day it may be connected to the Connally Ranch by trail. Also on the wish list is a permanent home for the Carolyn Parr Museum.

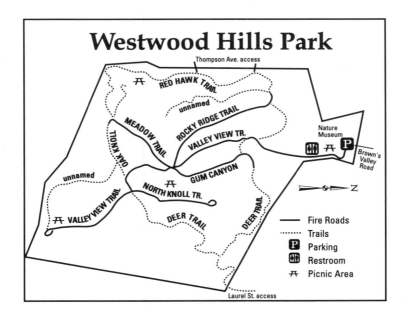

Westwood Hills Park

Thompson Ave. access

RED HAWK TRAIL

unnamed

ROCKY RIDGE TRAIL

MEADOW TRAIL

VALLEY VIEW TR.

OAK TRAIL

Nature Museum

Brown's Valley Road

unnamed

GUM CANYON

NORTH KNOLL TR.

VALLEY VIEW TRAIL

DEER TRAIL

DEER TRAIL

N

—— Fire Roads

········· Trails

P Parking

⑪ Restroom

ᚈ Picnic Area

Laurel St. access

TRAIL NOTES:

Westwood Hills is small enough (110 acres) that you'll be able to see it all in an hour's brisk walk. The described trail mainly uses the smaller trails and avoids all but short sections of roadway. Of course any combination of trails or roads may be taken.

Take the road (Valley View Trail) from the parking lot past a locked gate. The old farmhouse on your left is the original dwelling of the rancher who grazed cattle on this property. Young eucalyptus groves appear first on the right then on both sides. The fire of July 1976 killed most of these trees, some 200 feet tall. Almost everything here is regrowth. As you pass by a second gate, a water trough to the left is one used by cattle that graze park hills in the summer months. Vegetation turns native with bay and live oak overstory.

Immediately after a tall Monterey cypress and a resting bench, turn right on an unnamed trail at ¼ mile. Soon you pass a third gate. This section of trail was built by a young man in a wheelchair. Just below the top of the knoll the trail appears to veer right, but it soon leads into private property. **Turn left** (at the time of this writing a large tree blocked the path. This confusing junction is top priority for the next Scout trail project). Continue up through oak, bay and madrone with lots of poison oak underfoot.

Come to a trail junction at ⅜ mile. Turn left briefly onto Rocky Ridge Trail and pass a fourth gate. Soon take the first unmarked right turn onto the Red Hawk Trail. At another signed trail junction stay right and head downhill. A stone wall plunges toward Thompson Street. Hand-built walls like these were made between 100 and 150 years ago, both to clear fields of rocks and serve as property boundaries. At ½ mile descend wooden steps placed by inmates (they do much trail and fire work in the county). Watch for wildflowers in spring at an open meadow. In winter this hillside is running with water and slippery. Near the park's west boundary a trail leads to one of the two entrances on

Thompson Avenue.

A concrete-pipe bridge at ⅝ mile crosses a small creek. To the left a live oak has sent a limb snaking along the ground for forty feet in search of sun. You soon arrive at the other Thompson Avenue entrance. This was once the only entrance to the park. There is what looks like the remains of a stone cistern. After a short climb, traverse a grassy hill veering first south then east. A llama often grazes in the field to the south.

The Red Hawk Trail ends beyond ¾ mile. To the left is Oak Knoll, with a picnic table under graceful oaks. At one time the ten acres around it was the only land proposed as a park. Turn right onto Oak Knoll Trail through the finest oak woodland in the park. Soon come to a signed trail junction. Oak Knoll goes left. Stay right on an unnamed trail and go steeply uphill to a meadow. The narrow, stony trail ahead was cut by volunteers with hand chisels. Use caution here in winter when it's wet.

At 1 mile turn left up wooden steps at the fence boundary. On your left is an awesome live oak estimated at 300 years old. Three of its huge limbs have sagged to the ground for some distance. Cows like it under here. For some reason, their altar-shaped cow patty piles have a vague ceremonial look about them. The trail rises steeply to the ridgetop past a tree restoration project.

Soon you reach Hilltop, high point of the park. This used to be a 360 degree view, but a mansion now blocks the sight of San Francisco and the Golden Gate Bridge. Although the Spanish tile roof and whitewashed walls would be attractive in a neighborhood, it is an out-of-place eyesore in this location. That goes double for the communications towers.

Still visible are three landmarks of the Bay Area — Mount St. Helena, Mount Tamalpais and Mount Diablo. Almost the whole town of Napa is laid out below. Down the hill east might be seen cattle of the owner who has grazing rights to the park. A bench and table are provided for rest and/or picnicking.

Now back on Valley View Trail, walk along the level top, then drop to a three-trail junction beyond 1¼ miles where a graffitti-scrawled picnic table and trash can are chained to a dying madrone. Take the right fork, walking on narrow Deer Trail under an arched tree branch. Soon Mount George (1,877 feet) looms due east. The steep hillside trail takes you past a draw with a buckeye grove.

Begin the steep descent near an oak stump, passing bare hillside to an unmarked trail junction. To the right a trail leads to a fourth park entrance/exit at Laurel Street. Continue straight and come to so-called Cardboard Hill, a dirt hillside on the right where kids used to ride homemade sleds. Re-enter an oak forest where a barbed wire fence is close enough to tear your clothes.

A trail junction with Gum Canyon is at 1¾ miles. Stay right on Deer Trail, head slightly uphill and then left at an arrowed sign. In this area is the remains of a stone pond used to water cattle. Soon you arrive at the junction with Valley View Trail. Turn right and go ¼ mile to the parking lot for a total distance of just over 2 miles.

NAPA RIVER TRAIL

River front access on an old historic waterway

Nathan Coombs chose the site for the city of Napa for one reason — it was as far upriver as large boats could navigate. The burgeoning river commerce that Coombs foresaw fostered Napa for half a century. The river then sustained another fifty years of neglect and abuse. As we near the millennium, long range plans for the river's renewal and care are going through a protracted birth. The Napa Urban Waterfront Restoration Plan, a combination of flood control, river front development and riparian renewal may one day make Napans proud again of their historic waterway.

Native Americans lived along the river for thousands of years, using boats made of tule reeds to fish and to cross from one bank to the other. Two tribes, the Wappo and Patwin, both lived in the vicinity of present day Napa. The tribal boundary line was roughly the confluence of Napa Creek and Napa River, with the Wappo north of there, the Patwin south.

Indians were still very much a presence in 1836 when Nicolas Higuera was granted *Rancho Entre Napa* by Mexico. It included that land which is now the city of Napa and the Carneros to the west. Nathan Coombs was only twenty-two when he received land along the river in exchange for building a barn for Higuera. Coombs founded Napa in 1848

— the same year James Marshall found gold in Coloma.

Often men who failed to find gold in the Sierra struck it rich in Napa. They bought cheap valley land and raised crops from deep, virgin, volcanic soil. They raised cattle for hides and tallow — Napa's first industry — or grew wheat and fruit. As San Francisco blossomed, Napa farmers and ranchers supplied the city with its bounty. No all-year roads existed, nor bridges over the river. There was only one highway in those days — the river.

Located where the river was navigable at low tide, the town of Suscol, founded by Mariano Vallejo, was competitive with Napa for a short time. The first ferry operated there by 1852, connecting the Sacramento–Petaluma overland stage route. Steamships would bring visitors and tourists from San Francisco who disembarked at Suscol to take stage, and later, rail service to up-valley resorts.

Heavy industry, though, favored Napa. Tanneries, lumber yards, gas works and warehouses full of grain, apples and wine lined the river front for miles. As many as seven different wharves operated at one time. The work horse of the river was the scow schooner, built to carry heavy loads and move quickly, rarely drafting more than twenty-two inches of water. These boats took local agricultural goods — oats, wheat, corn, puncheons of wine and hides to San Francisco and returned with finished products — machinery, tools, and sewer pipes.

Lumber schooners designed to sail the open sea brought in lumber from Mendocino mills and left with tan bark from the forests of Mount St. Helena. As many as fifty ships a day jostled for space on the Napa River.

Napa prospered. Wealthy merchants and river captains built Victorian mansions which still stand near Division Street. They simply walked out their front door to work. The river-driven economy lasted until Henry Ford's invention, when roads and bridges made access to Napa easy. The era closed when the steamship *Zinfandel* made its last run in 1920.

Abuse of the waterway followed neglect. The river served as an unofficial trash dump, while sewer lines emptied directly into the river. Amazingly, the only other water source for Napa until 1924, besides backyard wells, was the Napa River itself. A small dam backed up a quarter mile-long lake just upstream from the Trancas Bridge. Water was filtered through an old locomotive boiler filled with sand. Poor water quality, brackish and black with manganese and iron, plus lack of water pressure in the mains, brought the swift completion of Milliken Dam in the eastern hills.

Mare Island Naval Base revitalized a slumping Napa economy by 1941, doubling then redoubling the population. Increasing abuse of the river wasn't addressed until 1948 when Napa Sanitation District was formed. Many residents remember the river so toxic it would kill fish by the thousands and peel paint off nearby buildings. By 1953, storm and sewer lines were separated and the river began to heal.

Out of a flood control proposal in the early 1960s has grown a multiple purpose environmental project, the Napa Urban Waterfront Restoration Plan. A phalanx of federal, state and local agencies are involved. Flood control will be accomplished by a variety of methods including widening and deepening the channel, construction of earth levees, concrete and sheet pile flood walls, habitat restoration, and bypass of the oxbow. Fishermen will have improved access with six new piers. Hikers and bicyclists will have six miles of trail on the west bank of the river to enjoy, from John F. Kennedy Park on the south end to Trancas Street on the north. Parks and Recreation has plans to connect the river trail with other regional trails like the Bay Area Ridge Trail, the Bay Trail, and Napa Valley Trail (along the river to Calistoga).

A new respect is emerging for our waterways and wetlands. Although only one eighth of Napa County's original wetlands remain, conservationists are striving to save what's left. Recently 9,850 acres of the Napa Marsh were purchased through Proposition 117 funds. The marshes are important wintering habitat for twenty-five species of Pacific flyway waterfowl. Twelve thousand canvasbacks have been seen at a time.

The Napa River remains one of the best steelhead streams in the Bay Area, with spawning on Redwood, Brown's Valley, Milliken, Tulocay and Napa creeks. The rare Mason's quillwort (*Lilaeopsis masonii*) may be found on old pilings in the Napa River and along Old Tulocay Creek. In recent years, a sea lion, a gray whale and a river otter have been spotted frolicking in these waters. With understanding of its past, and care for its future, the Napa River may emerge from its tarnished image to reclaim a place in the hearts of Napans.

TRANCAS to LINCOLN SEGMENT

DIRECTIONS: From Highway 29 in Napa drive east on Trancas Street 1.5 miles, or .5 mile from the Silverado Trail. Look for the hiker access sign on the west side of the Napa River.

DISTANCE: 1¼ miles one way

GRADE: Easy. Mostly level walking.

BEST TIME: All year

INFO: Napa Parks and Recreation, 707/257-9529

WARNING: The only officially dedicated parts of this trail are short segments near Trancas and near Lincoln. The rest is social trail. The elderly, the very young and the handicapped may find rough going in places. Some parts of the trail may be ponded in winter.

TRAIL NOTES:

Your trail starts as a wide path of crushed granite. Housing tracts on the west will accompany you the whole way.

The river bank is wild with native and introduced species — blackberry, ivy, periwinkle and wild grape — under live oak and bay.

Before ¼ mile the path turns to packed earth and narrows. Here is the first of four access points to Soscol Avenue. This part can be muddy and slippery in winter. The river may be flowing disconcertingly upstream if the tide is in. Soon come to a large shady clearing where an oversize barbecue pit sits behind the Napa Elks Lodge. Detour left around this low spot in winter, then go up wooden steps to the embankment top.

At ⅜ mile is a second access to Soscol. Young bike riders use a series of dirt hummocks along the trail as a fun obstacle course. Embankments have been built to protect houses from flooding. At ½ mile the slightly elevated view of the river is a good place for photographs.

A third public access to Soscol Avenue is at ⅝ mile. Bird life is abundant along the river — in the bush will be robins, jays, finches, quail and juncos while in the tree tops are owls, red-tailed hawks, crows and vultures. The trail widens and terrain opens beyond ⅝ mile. At ¾ mile a bridge supporting a large water pipe, now in disuse, crosses the Napa River.

You soon pass the fourth and final access to Soscol. Forests of fennel stand ten feet high while next to the river stately cottonwoods appear. At mile 1 you pass a gate, locked at sunset, and the path is once again crushed granite. Skirt the Outdoor Resorts of America RV Park under cover of live oak and bay. This is perhaps the best river photo opportunity on the trail. Your peaceful walk ends before 1¼ miles with the roar of Lincoln Avenue traffic.

KENNEDY PARK SEGMENT

DIRECTIONS: From Highway 29 take Imola Avenue east to Soscol Avenue. Turn right. Just past Napa Valley College turn right again on Streblow Drive. Follow it past the golf course, over the railroad tracks, then veer left to the boat launch area.

DISTANCE: ⅞ mile one way

GRADE: Easy. All level walking.

BEST TIME: Winter for birding. All year for walking.

INFO: Napa Parks and Recreation, 707/257-9529

SUGGESTION: Bring binoculars for viewing bird life.

WARNING: Only ¼ mile of this trail by the waterfowl pond is officially dedicated. The rest of the levee may be rough walking for some.

TRAIL NOTES:

Begin at the boat launch pier and go right (north). At the interpretive display case the road forks left. As you approach the river notice the smell of the sea! The large open field across the river is the Stewart Ranch. In the eastern foothills is Basalt Rock Quarry and above it Skyline Park.

Walk ¼ mile along the earthen levee to an excellent display case with extensive information on birds including the endangered California clapper rail. To the east is a newly created lake that may hold seagulls, coots, pintails, mallards, canvasback, and geese. It is connected to the river by a strategically placed under-road pipe. There is a constant flow of water between the two bodies of water, depending on the tide, so the lake water is always fresh.

A trail fork leads to the right to another access point. Continue along the river as the road turns to pavement. You will likely see fishermen all along the river. They are here for sturgeon, striped bass (striper), flounder, and mudsuckers (used for bait). One fisherman told me his luck was best with the tide flowing in. Sturgeon, an ancient fish, is the prize catch. The species on the Pacific coast is Sacramento sturgeon (*Acipenser transmontanus*) individuals attaining an age of 200–300 years and weighing up to 818 kilograms (1800 pounds). Fisherman may keep only those between four and six feet long, which translates to under a hundred pounds.

Another popular activity is flying remote-control airplanes. Pilots use the same field (west of the college) where the northern harrier and the black-shouldered kite are commonly seen. The black-shouldered kite, like the kestrel, likes to hover over open fields in search of prey. You might also see the sharp-shinned hawk, Cooper's hawk, and yellow warblers in the trees along the earthen levee.

Across the river at ¾ mile is a boat marina. Soon the Maxwell Bridge comes into view, the big green drawbridge on Imola Avenue. At ⅞ mile the public road ends. Just over the railroad tracks is an old brick building said to have been a pump house when Napa State Hospital owned it. Beyond is restricted access to the college. Return the same way.

ADDITIONAL HIKING:

From the boat launch a trail goes left along the river bank for ¾ mile. It comes to an abrupt end with a twenty-foot drop to the river (careful here, the ground you stand on today could be at the bottom of San Pablo Bay tomorrow). Across an artificially enlarged tributary is the old Kaiser Steel works (now Napa Steel Company). You can return the same way or take a volunteer trail east until you get to a levee top bordering the golf course. Before that, you pass an old tug boat in decay. Take the levee back to the parking lot, keeping an eye out for badly hooked (or sliced) golf balls.

SKYLINE WILDERNESS PARK

Former state hospital grounds offer the most hiking in the county

DIRECTIONS: In the city of Napa, from Highway 221 or Highway 29, take Imola Avenue east to its end at Fourth Avenue.
FEE: $4 per vehicle
BEST TIME: Spring
INFO: Skyline Park, 707/252-0481

In October 1841, Cayetano Juarez received the Mexican Land Grant he called *Rancho Tulocay*. Located east of the present city of Napa, it included the land where Napa Valley College and Napa State Hospital are today. The Old Adobe Hut is part of the original Juarez home and still stands on Soscol Avenue. Juarez sold a portion of his ranch to the State of California in 1873. It included those lands occupied by the College, Kennedy Park and Napa State Hospital.

When the Napa Asylum for the Insane arose in 1875, it was the most impressive building in the state. The Gothic Farmhouse was said to be a mile in circumference, made of slate, marble and nine million bricks made on site. It was five stories high, decorated with gargoyles and crowned with seven towers, the highest 175 feet tall. Called domestic Gothic by its architect, later generations perceived it as scary European medieval. The causes of insanity were not well understood then. Patients were admitted for such reasons as business problems, religion and trouble in love.

Funds for maintenance were limited, so a mammoth agricultural operation was instigated to help defray costs. The 500 patients raised vegetable crops, worked the orchards and vineyards, and tended dairy herds and pigs. Some patients were admitted for marginal reasons and cured readily. Some of these were poor, without homes or families, and once released had nowhere to go. Thus began the tradition of former patients living in the woods of present Skyline Park.

Between 1876 and 1881 land behind the hospital was bought from William Coombs, brother of Napa's founder Nathan Coombs. The first structure built by the hospital in 1873, the small Coombs Ranch Dam, was no longer supplying sufficient water for the growing hospital. In the next ten years, Lake Louise, Lake Camille, and Lake Como were built for both practical and aesthetic reasons. The final property purchases in 1906 and 1908 took the hospital lands to the Solano County line. They were bought expressly to build another reservoir, Lake Marie. This was finished in two stages for $91,000 and became the main water supply.

Before World War II it was popular with automobile owners to take a drive through the grounds for picnicking and swimming. The hospital had its own post office, and mail was often addressed to Imola, California. The name appears to come from Italy, the center of that country's mental institutions.

Social and economic forces that changed so many things after World War II also came to Napa State Hospital. Local business groups complained that farm therapy, in which patients worked the land for free, was unfair competition. Treatment of patients had changed radically, modern drug therapy bringing care indoors. And the hospital, not intended for use day and night, was badly overcrowded. In 1949 it was declared unfit for human habitation and torn down after seventy-six years of service. Demolition was mostly by wrecking ball, but for the rock-solid main tower the workmen had to resort to dynamite.

In 1969 the State of California had no more use for the wild lands behind the hospital and announced intentions to sell to private buyers. Environmentalists had a better idea and begged the county for a park. The county refused, but a novel idea emerged. By 1978 the Skyline Park Citizens Committee was leasing the land from the county, who in turn had a lease from the state, a unique solution.

The 850-acre park opened in May 1983. With minimal government funding, Skyline Park Citizens Association has run the park on a shoestring budget raised by user fees, fundraisers and private donations, all on volunteer effort. Other groups supporting this arrangement are horse clubs, archers, bicycle clubs and the Native Plant Society.

The park today features fifteen miles of hiking on twelve trails, from old-growth oak woodland on hilltops to sunny meadows full of wildflowers in the spring, to cool streamside pleasure under bay and alder canopy. Wildlife includes deer, coyote, large flocks of wild turkey, wild pig and birds of prey. Near the entrance are a native plant garden, RV campground, archery range and community hall.

LAKE MARIE ROAD

Skyline's most popular trail

DISTANCE:	2 miles one way (add ⅜ mile to get to trailhead from entrance)
GRADE:	Easy
ELEVATION GAIN:	650 feet

TRAIL NOTES:

From the parking lot's south corner take the signed trail, then turn to the right before the native plant garden. Take the grassy path west to a road and turn left. Follow the fenced corridor between Lake Camille and Lake Louise. The odd structure on your left, looking like a stone crypt, was once the pumping plant for now dry Lake Como on your right. You soon arrive at the start of Skyline, Buckeye and Lake Marie trails.

Go left on the rocky and rutted road you may share with horses and bike riders. On your left is Camp Coombs, still

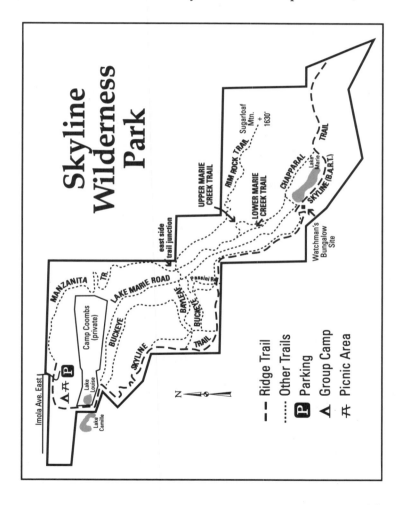

Skyline Wilderness Park

- — Ridge Trail
⋯⋯ Other Trails
🅿 Parking
▲ Group Camp
⊼ Picnic Area

part of Napa State Hospital. These fruit and nut trees — peach, fig, olive and walnut — were once tended by hospital patients. Great masses of striped white eyes and seepspring monkeyflowers grow on the thin-soil hillsides in spring.

The road climbs steeply to a trail junction with a piped-spring horse trough at ¼ mile. Lower Marie Creek Trail at this time is overgrown and not recommended. Oakleaf Trail climbs the hill briefly then parallels Lake Marie road for ½ mile before joining again. Continue straight past a shallow, fern-rimmed cave that most likely was dug for water exploration.

The steep climb proffers a bench for the weary at ½ mile, then a view of striking cliff formations in Marie Creek. These are known locally as Little Yosemite. Top the hill at ⅝ mile. The red wooden structure up the hill to your right is a wildlife viewing platform built by the Boy Scouts. A lengthy stone wall descends from it , and, in broken fashion, crosses the creek and climbs the eastern hillside. Although no one knows for certain, it may be stonework from the nineteenth century to mark property boundaries. These are found in many parts of the park.

Water exploration cave

Descending, you pass the Oakleaf Trail junction and leave the city noise of Napa behind. The Bayleaf Trail joins at ⅞ mile and across from here is the enormous, venerable Fig Tree. This edible fig creates its own microclimate with a ground-to-ground canopy. It's probably one hundred years old.

Just uphill is the best picnic site in the park. A table under a big oak overlooks a meadow with at least one Indian grinding rock. Through the meadow and across the creek are Manzanita, Rim Rock and Marie Creek trails. Continue on Marie Lake Road past the Passini Road junction at mile 1 (Passini Road is a right-of-way out of the park). Stone wall remnants abound here. Descend into shadier oak/bay woodland.

A cave just beyond has a charming waterfall in the winter. The cave goes back at least twenty feet, with standing water on the cave floor. The vegetation becomes lush at 1¼ miles. Down in the creek are alder trees up to one hundred feet tall. The next ¼ mile holds the strangest and most mysterious sights in Skyline. Weird ruins reminiscent of ancient Egypt, or Mayan temples moldering in tropical jungles come to mind. Historians still haven't found the answers to their origin.

Down in Marie Creek is the only redwood in the park. It was introduced, since redwoods don't occur here naturally. The forest is dense with oak, madrone and soaring columns of bay laurel. At 1⅞ miles an unmarked road leads left to a meadow and picnic table at the base of the earthen dam (no need to conjure images of the San Francisquito dam disaster of 1925 while eating lunch here. The dam is considered safe and as an extra precaution the lake level was lowered permanently after 1986). Immediately beyond are two connectors with Skyline Trail, one signed.

Reach Lake Marie, your destination, at mile 2. There is a crossbar to tie your horse to, a bench and a trash can, I guess for those whose empty lunch sacks are too heavy to carry out. Swimming isn't allowed here but the bass fishing is said to be excellent.

RIM ROCK TRAIL

Best views in the park

DISTANCE: 1¾ miles one way (to get to the trailhead, add 1 mile via Lake Marie Road, 1⅝ miles by the Manzanita Trail)

GRADE: Moderate

ELEVATION GAIN: 1,500 feet

TRAIL NOTES:

Follow the sign with the arrow that says SUGARLOAF (it will be replaced with a better sign with the words Rim Rock Trail). Go through a gap in the stone wall, then turn right before the chain link fence. Ascend gradually through manzanita and oak. The trail mostly avoids a thicket of chamise, and rewards you with a view into beautiful Marie Canyon after ¼ mile.

The trail starts to climb steeply and as you approach the ½-mile mark, Mount Veeder appears to the west, and beyond it, parts of Sonoma County. As you leave oak woodland, red volcanic rock outcroppings rise above the trail. From here, Mount Cobb to the northwest in Lake County is seen juxtaposed with Mount St. Helena.

At ¾ mile you skirt the headwaters of a very small canyon with fine old coast live oak overhead. A series of steep switchbacks begin and soon you are high enough to see Mount Tamalpais in Marin County. In late afternoon, sunlight glinting golden off the rivers, bays and estuaries give the serpentine complex of San Pablo Bay a rare beauty.

The trail becomes indistinct at 1¼ miles at a classic oak and grass hilltop. Look for a rock cairn, or, if missing, a coast live oak with a large branch growing horizontally west. At this point head north uphill to a faint trail fork. This next stretch of trail was unfinished in summer 1995. Take either fork northeast to the hilltop.

The trail improves in 300 feet and so does the view. This

is the best view in the park. All of Napa Valley from the foot of Mount St. Helena to the San Pablo Bay is visible. You can trace fifty miles of the Napa River from its source to its end at Mare Island Strait. Bring your panorama camera for this one. On a crystal clear day San Francisco and the Golden Gate Bridge look within paraglider range.

Near the top the trail levels out for easier walking. Before 1¾ miles you'll see a hilltop microwave station to the northeast. This is East Sugarloaf (1,686 feet). The trail peters out anticlimactically on West Sugarloaf (1,630 feet) on a wooded hill. The trail will one day take a loop back, but for now, return the same way.

SKYLINE TRAIL

The first dedicated section of Bay Area Ridge Trail in the North Bay

DISTANCE:	3½ miles one way (from the parking lot it is 8+ miles round trip)
GRADE:	Strenuous
ELEVATION GAIN:	1,000 feet

TRAIL NOTES:

After the ⅜-mile approach, turn right at the three-way trailhead junction. To the right is dry Lake Como, created by an earthen levee in 1890. It was once fed by springs that have vanished. Soon you come upon monumental piles of old rusting food tins. The open maw of the quarry looms to the south. It was originally a state hospital operation but has been leased to Basalt Rock for many years.

After ⅛ mile pass by the bike and horse alternate trail and come to the Skyline turnoff. Turn left and immediately the trail narrows and climbs steeply. The well constructed trail ascends a rocky meadow in sweeping curves. On the fringes are groves of buckeye, oak and bay. Many seeps and springs water a colorful variety of native wildflowers in spring. In winter the quarry becomes a lake.

Starting at ½ mile, each westerly bend of the trail contacts a stone wall, built in the nineteenth century ranching days. This is the longest stone wall in the park, one which you will see for two miles. Go through an opening in a redwood stake fence and look on the left for a grand old oak 200 to 300 years old.

Leave the oak grassland behind at ¾ mile and enter mixed evergreen forest. Trailside poison oak is rank. The steepest part of the Skyline Trail soon ends after climbing 600 vertical feet. At the stone wall the trail makes a right angle turn southeast. There is a fine grassy picnic area under oak and bay but watch for poison oak. Beyond the wall are views of the Napa Marsh and Mount Tamalpais. Pass by the Bayleaf Trail junction on the left and go downhill through a small jumble of rocks.

At mile 1 a short connector goes left to join the Buckeye and Bayleaf Trails. Stay right. The stone wall you parallel separates two distinct properties — the park with its fine stands of oak, the other (when I went through) with its several burn piles of oaks. The live oaks here may be the finest in the park. White-flowered toothwort, called the first wildflower of spring, may appear among the grasses in the dead of winter.

The large meadow at 1¼ miles holds many rodents to attract such raptors as the red-tailed and sharp-shinned hawks and the kestrel. The stone wall splits into two segments and gracefully disappears over the hills south and southeast. Stay right at another connector to the Buckeye Trail. Mount George and West Sugarloaf to the northeast and Mount Veeder and Mount St. John to the west are your landmarks. The trail veers off the crest to climb a hill of chaparral with coffeeberry and coyote brush.

Begin a major nosedive at 1½ miles and cross Passini Road before 1¾ miles. Follow the sign that points uphill. Round the shoulder and traverse precipitous cliffs of Marie Creek Canyon. You come to a confusing three-way junction. To the left is a connector to the Buckeye Trail. The right fork is blocked by logs. Take the middle fork uphill, parallel a fence south, and soon top out into magnificent oak grassland. In the vicinity of mile 2 are ancient live oaks 300 to 400 years old. Just beyond is a huge bay laurel with a dozen trunks from half a foot to 1½ feet in diameter each.

Stay right at the Buckeye Trail junction at 2¼ miles and enter dense oak/bay forest with wood fern understory. Stay right again at a connector to the Lake Marie Road and come to the remains of the so-called Sea Captain's House at 2⅜ miles. The cottage may once have been a superintendent's retreat but by 1918 it was referred to as the Watchman's Bungalow. The keeper of the dam lived here, enjoying a view of the lake from his wraparound porch. By 1920 when his duties ended, it was dismantled and rebuilt on the hospital grounds.

Stay to the right at another connector to Lake Marie Road. Follow an old roadbed around the lake. The hillside is a solid mass of wood ferns. At 2½ miles is the last connec-

Lake Louise

tor to Lake Marie Road. Cross Marie Creek above the lake inlet at 2⅞ miles with giant alders overhead. Take note of the Chaparral Trail junction soon after — it's a good loop return. For the first time, you are at creek level, the bay/alder riparian overstory always cool on a hot day. Cross a series of sloping meadows where the trail is a muddy mess in winter from horse, bike, and hiker traffic. The trail ends at 3½ miles at a locked gate.

It is planned, one day, for the Bay Area Ridge Trail to continue on to Green Valley, Rockville Hills Park and Benecia.

ADDITIONAL TRAILS

MANZANITA TRAIL

DISTANCE: 1⅝ miles one way
GRADE: Easy
BEST TIME: Winter, spring

The trail begins just beyond the park entrance by the kiosk. It skirts the archery range and Camp Coombs, then follows south-facing chaparral slopes to the east side trails junction. It can be uncomfortably warm in summer.

TOYON TRAIL

DISTANCE: 1¼ miles one way
GRADE: Easy
BEST TIME: Winter, spring

Take Manzanita Trail ⅓ mile to the turnoff. This short, vague overgrown section rejoins Manzanita after ¼ mile. Continue on Manzanita/Toyon to ⅝ mile. At this point you are above the housing at Camp Coombs. Look closely for the unsigned Toyon Trail marked by a blue ribbon. Go right and downhill following other blue ribbon markers. Before ¾ mile ignore another trail blocked by brush that leads downhill to Camp Coombs and private property. From here the Toyon Trail should be clearer. You pass above Little Yosemite and join Manzanita Trail at 1¼ miles.

BUCKEYE TRAIL

DISTANCE: 2 miles one way
GRADE: Moderate
BEST TIME: All year

Take the fenced corridor between Lakes Camille and Louise to the three-way trail junction. Buckeye Trail traverses north-facing hillsides and joins Skyline Trail before Lake Marie. It is a well designed and maintained trail featuring a remarkable buckeye forest, beautiful open meadow and steep fern-covered canyon walls. This is one of my favorites.

OAKLEAF TRAIL

DISTANCE: ½ mile one way
GRADE: Easy

From the trailhead, take Lake Marie Road ¼ mile to the junction. Oakleaf Trail rejoins Lake Marie road before the Fig Tree.

BAYLEAF TRAIL

DISTANCE: ⅝ mile one way
GRADE: Easy
BEST TIME: Spring, summer

Take Lake Marie Road ⅞ mile to the junction near the Fig Tree. Bayleaf is a moderate climb beside an intermittent

stream through oak/bay woodland. Lake Marie/Bayleaf/
Skyline trails make a fine 2½-mile loop.

PASSINI ROAD

DISTANCE: ⅓ mile one way

Take Lake Marie Road 1 mile. Passini is a badly eroded
right-of-way into private property. It can be used as a good
connector to the Skyline Trail if you wish to avoid that trail's
initial steep climb.

UPPER MARIE CREEK TRAIL

DISTANCE: 1 ⅛ miles one way
GRADE: Moderate
BEST TIME: Spring, summer, fall

Take either Manzanita Trail, Toyon Trail or Lake Marie
Road to the start of Upper Marie Creek Trail at the east side
trail junction. Follow the creek, then turn left and uphill at
½ mile. A fine rocky knoll-top meadow with buckeye and
scrub oak perched above Marie Creek Canyon at ¾ mile
offers a good picnic site. At mile 1 an unmarked junction
leads you left on Chaparral Trail or right across the old
spillway to the dam top.

LOWER MARIE CREEK TRAIL
from east side junction
*(Lower Marie Creek from Lake Marie Road to the east side
trail junction,overgrown at time of writing, is not recommended,
and not described here.)*

DISTANCE: ¾ mile one way
GRADE: Moderate

BEST TIME: Spring, summer, fall. In winter creek crossings may be washed out.

Take Manzanita Trail, Toyon Trail or Lake Marie Road to east side trail junction. Follow same route as for Upper Marie Creek Trail for ½ mile, then bear right to continue along the creek. After the fourth creek crossing at ¾ mile a sign points uphill. The trail will become faint. Stay right at a faint connector path, then join the Upper Marie Creek Trail. From here it is ⅛ mile to Chaparral Trail.

CHAPARRAL TRAIL

DISTANCE: ⅜ mile one way
GRADE: Easy

Take either Marie Creek Trail or Lake Marie Road to the dam. It is signed only at the north end of the dam top. This short, narrow and, in places, rough trail affords the best view of Lake Marie. Use caution on steep slopes and slick rock. It connects with Skyline Trail above the lake inlet.

ROCKVILLE HILLS REGIONAL PARK

Historic cattle ranch is now a multi-use park

DIRECTIONS: From the south take Interstate 80 to Suisun Valley Road near Fairfield. Travel north to Rockville Road. Turn left (west) and go about a mile to the main entrance. A second entrance is .25 mile up Rockville Road.

A charming alternate from Napa takes the Monticello Road (Highway 121) to Wooden Valley Road, which becomes Suisun Valley Road, then meets Rockville Road.

HOURS: Dawn to dusk

DISTANCE: A perimeter loop is about 4½ to 5 miles. If you're the compulsive type and assiduously hike every trail, it would be 9 miles.

GRADE: Easy to moderate

BEST TIME: All year. Spring for wildflowers.

INFO: Rockville Hills Regional Park, 707/421-1351

SUGGESTION: Rockville is mountain biking heaven but bikers are stressing the park's resources. Please stay off areas under renovation; bikes do long term damage both off trail, and to rain-soaked trails. Consider a voluntary two-day ban on biking after big storms to prevent future mandatory measures.

Roy Mason knows cows. His family has run cattle in the Green Valley area since 1932. Besides owning vast acreage, he has grazing rights to the park during winter months. Mason likes to emphasize that well managed cattle do no harm to the land. Cows tend to contour graze a hillside. A good rancher will encourage this with contour fencing. But don't they eat the wildflowers, you say? On the contrary, the best place for wildflowers is thin, rocky soils where grass cover grows thinly. Thick grass cover will compete with flowers for sunlight and nutrients. For evidence, come out to Rockville Hills in March, April and May. The park has spectacular displays of nearly one hundred wildflower species. The key factor for abundant wildflowers is the quantity and timing of winter rains, the heavier and earlier the better.

According to Mason, his father bought several thousand acres from the Pierce family, one of the largest California landowners at the time, who went broke in the depression. About 1934 the Masons constructed a levee and the large stock pond was created. A right-of-way for the large utility towers you see on the property was granted before World War II. Every winter woodcutters lived on the property in small cabins to cut firewood. Cutting was selective, and done solely with hand tools. Some of the old hollow stumps are still visible. Of the very large trees, only their branches were cut. A keen eye can spot these regrowths today.

In the late 1950s a developer envisioned Rockville as a golf course. Irrigation lines were laid and two pumps were installed at the lower stock pond. Public sympathies for open space prevailed, and the property was sold to the City of Fairfield in 1968. Rockville Hills is now a popular regional park, having up to 400 people visit on a busy weekend day. One and a half miles of trail from the North Trailhead to the Green Valley Trailhead is dedicated as part of the Bay Area Ridge Trail system.

TRAIL NOTES:

Rockville's many trails lend themselves to wandering at will and whim. Most people take the road to the upper lake (½ mile) in the center of the park. A near perfect place for a picnic, it has several tables placed around the lake shore. High tension transmission towers are the only things that seem out of place. The lake is surrounded by grass hills peppered with blue oak and buckeye. Waterfowl like geese,

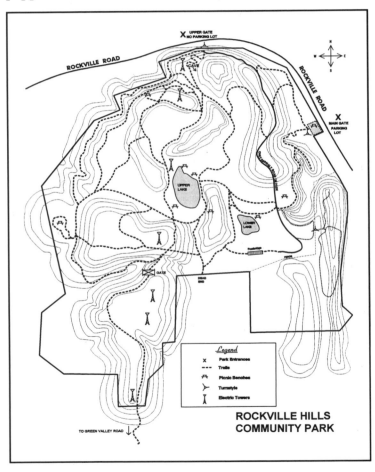

ROCKVILLE HILLS COMMUNITY PARK

mallards and coots glide the shallow water. From here trails branch everywhere.

The west side of the park is a bit more remote, more lush than most west-facing hillsides in California. Look for large specimens of live oak and black oak, views of Green Valley, Elkhorn Peak, and Twin Sisters on Vaca Ridge. A well preserved stone fence is part of the northern park boundary. Underneath volcanic cliffs pocked with caves is lush undergrowth laced with poison oak (one old oak was choked with the largest poison oak trunk I've ever seen, about one half foot in diameter).

As with Rome, all trails lead to the lake. Even for those with no sense of direction, it's impossible to get lost for long, so relax and enjoy.

Hikers pass under gnarled limb

STEBBINS COLD CANYON RESERVE

A part of the University of California Natural Reserve System

DIRECTIONS: From Rutherford take Highway 128, or from Napa take Highway 121 to Moskowite Corners. Continue on Highway 128 to Monticello Dam. After a short descent, at a sweeping bend in the road, Cold Creek passes under Cold Creek Bridge. Park at a large turnout on the left (north). The trail starts at an unlocked metal gate on the south side of the road.

DISTANCE: 1⅜ miles one way

GRADE: Moderate

BEST TIME: Spring, fall

INFO: U.C. Davis, 916/752-0649

WARNING: Area subject to mud slides in winter

Kentucky pioneer John Reid Wolfskill took possession of *Rancho Rio De Los Putos* near Winters in 1842. Part of his land extended along Putah Creek close to Devil's Gate, but Cold Canyon was just outside the rancho boundaries. Because he refused to become a Mexican citizen, the grant was actually made in his brother William's name. John Wolfskill was the founder of the horticulture industry in the Sacramento Valley. Some of his original fruit tree cuttings came from George Yount's *Rancho Caymus*.

A year later the Berryessa brothers, Jose and Sisto, were given their own Mexican land grant of 35,000 acres, later known as the *Rancho de las Putas*. It was the largest piece of land ever given in Napa County, covering most of Berryessa Valley. According to California historian Erwin Gudde, the Indian name *Putah* preserves the name of the branch of Patwin Indians who lived on its banks. He states that its similarity to the Spanish word *puta* (meaning harlot) is purely coincidental. A contrasting story circulates that employees of the Berryessas would go down to Putah Canyon to purchase Indian women for trinkets. Legend has it that the brothers Berryessa lost their land (at 25 cents per acre) chiefly to horse-race gambling debts.

The principal owners by 1866 were John Lawley, William Hamilton and J.H. Bostwick who made a killing by subdividing Berryessa Valley into small farms. A portion in the south was set aside for a town. The building of Monticello began the same year when E.A. Peacock erected the first hotel. Soon there were homes, a blacksmith shop, two general stores, more hotels, saloons and a cemetery. Eventually this farming community held about 200 people.

Agricultural emphasis changed from cattle to wheat. Wheat grew fast and rich due to the climate and the valley's soil, fifty per cent of which was later rated as Class 1 Yolo loam (very fertile). Getting it to market was another matter. Only two roads led out of this isolated valley. One, often flooded in the wet months, went down narrow Putah Canyon to Winters and the Sacramento Valley. The other was a brutal, two-day haul by mule wagon to Napa.

California's agriculture began to diversify about the time the wheat market weakened in the 1880s. Farmers slowly changed over to fruit growing, chiefly pears and grapes, by 1920. A small scale oil drilling business was run in the 1920s by a man named Griffiths. He lost financial backers in the depression and the fledgling business never recovered.

In Cold Canyon, a Greek named Vlahos raised goats for cheese on 160 acres in the mid 1930s. The ruins of the workshop and cold storage house can still be seen near the end of the first trail.

In the late 1970s, Cold Canyon below Monticello Dam was acquired by the Department of Fish and Game and the University of California at Davis. It is now a multi-use area, allowing ecological study, hiking, picnicking, swimming and hunting (contact Fish and Game or Bureau of Land Management for hunting season information). Wildlife includes

The flooding of Berryessa Valley

"Under the swelling pressure of a skyrocketing birth rate, places for people to live and water for crops and factories has become critical. . . . bulldozers are only slightly slower than atomic bombs . . . the nature of destruction is not altered by calling it the price of progress. To witness population inflation of such proportions that ways of life are uprooted, fruiting trees sawed down, productive land inundated and bodies already buried forced out of the ground is to realize that as life teems so does death. And that man is the active agent of both." From the inside front cover of Death of a Valley, by Dorothea Lange and Pirkle Jones, a pictorial chronicle of the last year of Berryessa Valley.

It was common knowledge from the late 1800s that Devil's Gate at the head of Putah Canyon would make an ideal dam site. As early as 1906 engineers were casting covetous eyes that way. It wasn't until 1948 that a bill to authorize dam construction appeared before Congress. That bill never passed. But the Secretary of the Interior exercised his independent power and gave it the go ahead. It was the only federal dam project ever approved in this way. Strong objection and attempted litigation by Napa County was fruitless.

fox, deer, coyote, quail, wild turkey and several kinds of raptors.

TRAIL NOTES:

Once inside the unlocked metal gate there are two choices: Take the main trail veering right to the creek or an alternate trail straight ahead through a brushy meadow. The second choice takes you past a western redbud tree, loaded with thin red seed pods in winter. Toyon, coyote brush and

With tactics similar to the Owens Valley land buyout by Los Angeles at the turn of the century, federal authorities offered farmers prices far below market value for their property. Facing eminent domain, landowners in Berryessa Valley had little choice but to sell. Many would never find land again at comparable cost. During the final year of 1956, a few houses were moved to higher ground. The rest were burned. All trees were ordered cut to within six inches of the ground, including ancient valley oaks, landmarks for centuries to the Indians, Spanish and Americans. Bodies were disinterred from Monticello Cemetery and moved to Spanish Flat. The only structure left intact was the Putah Creek Bridge. Quarried from local sandstone, at 217 feet it was called the largest stone bridge west of the Rockies. Today it is buried under 160 feet of water.

Much to everyone's surprise, heavy rains quickly filled Berryessa Valley that first winter. Under the rising waters, one-sixth of Napa County's farming acreage disappeared. Tax revenues lost are estimated at $800,000 per year. Lake Berryessa is solely on Napa County land, yet none of its water benefitted the county (Solano County farms are the main beneficiaries). Although not an original objective, recreation soon became popular. Now bass fishing, water skiing, swimming, board sailing and house boating are enjoyed through the year.

poison oak grow beneath an overstory of oaks.

Descend a steep bank with wooden steps to an unnamed creek I jokingly call Gigolo Creek (companion to Putah Creek). Although its watershed is small, the floodwaters of 1995 raised hell here. Its vegetation and soil were stripped away, leaving the creek banks denuded, the old trail buried under tons of detritus.

Just beyond a second gate before ¼ mile you may sign the trail register and read about the reserve at an information display case. This is an ecological study area for students and teachers of U.C. Davis. Please leave study areas undisturbed. Soon you'll pass a tall, classic-looking gray pine. The trail negotiates a short hill. Water bars are placed diagonally to channel water off and avoid trail erosion.

The trail crosses another small hillock with water bars at ⅓ mile. It came down as a mud slide some years ago. In February shiny brown seeds of the buckeye will litter the

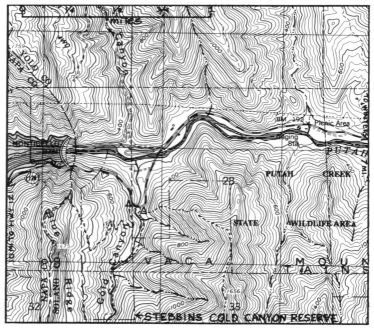

ground, sending out pale white roots.

At ½ mile there is another flood-ravaged tributary. Parallel the main creek to find the trail again. Look for newts (orange-bellied salamanders) here on overcast days in winter and early spring. All along the trail in spring are wildflowers — brodiaea, monkeyflower, Indian paintbrush, white-flowered yarrow and yerba santa, western wallflower and masses of golden fairy lantern.

Just before ¾ mile you come face to face with Cold Creek. In winter a few days may mean the difference between crossing and turning back. There is a good rock hop crossing fifty feet upstream on the left. On a warm day the plunge is better. At ⅞ mile the presence of a short wooden bridge across an insignificant stream is a mystery. Soon you come to a large mud slide, still oozing in February 1995.

Beyond 1 mile the trail climbs steadily above the creek, but heavy overgrowth of chaparral forces you to walk in a deep erosion gully, created despite regularly spaced water bars. The trail veers south to follow what looks like a tributary of Cold Creek. But a glance at the map shows you are still on Cold Creek. What's going on? Answer: a nomenclature anomaly. The larger Wild Horse Creek which joins Cold Creek below, has been given tributary status by mistake. According to standards set by the Geographic Board, the waters running into Putah Creek should be called Wild Horse Creek. Local usage and custom are so strong that to change back would only cause further confusion.

Before 1¼ miles cross beams on posts are engraved: "High Erosion Area, No Entry Please." It refers to badly eroded grassy hillsides to the west. Cross an erosion-damaged creek and arrive at a cleared area. A low stone wall is a remnant of an old homestead, perhaps a stock pen. By the creek grows an enormous, many-branched gray pine.

Soon you'll see, under a coast live oak, a stone foundation that was the goat farm workshop. Between the house and creek is a hole six feet deep lined with stones, perhaps a storage facility for perishables. Rusted metal junk covers

the bank, and across the trail is a bed frame with springs buried three-quarters sideways.

The trail soon narrows, crosses a small creek bed and descends to Cold Creek. Ford at 1⅓ miles and find a second foundation in somewhat better shape. This was the cold house where goat cheese was stored. Built partially underground and shaded by the dense canopy of oak and bay trees, it stayed remarkably cool through the summer. This is the end of the trail. However, it is easy to follow the stream another 500 feet to a charming waterfall.

ADDITIONAL TRAILS

Following are brief descriptions of two other trails available to hikers. They go to the east and west ridges of the watershed. Be aware that once on the ridgetops heading south, you are on Bureau of Land Management land, open to hunting all year.

EAST TRAIL:
Take the left fork at the trailhead and ascend two or

three switchbacks to a fence corner. Here the trail bolts straight up the spine of the ridge. The steep hillside's tall grass hides many wildflowers like lupine, yarrow, and brodiaea in spring. Pass groves of gray pine and blue oak, then two minor knolls and top out beyond ¾ mile by stepping through the basal ring of a fallen tree. View Monticello Dam and Lake Berryessa to the west, Winters and the Central Valley to the east.

Most people will want to stop here. But the trail does continue, taking a right-angle southerly tack, with rock hopping over poison oak-infested sandstone boulders. The level ridge is narrow and drops off steeply in places. The trail becomes badly overgrown at the base of a steep hill. If you're game, it, reportedly, goes another mile or so to an old orchard and Quonset hut.

WEST TRAIL:

This trail starts on the west side of Cold Creek at another metal gate. An enormous slide has taken out the road. Make your way over the hummocky mess that is difficult, but not too dangerous, to cross. The road gets better but is still marred by ruts up to two feet deep. It switchbacks steeply uphill for ¾ mile to an oak-rimmed meadow. To the west is an unstable sandstone cliff, known for rock fall in recent months.

The road turns to trail and charges up a steep, rocky and rutted hill. Soon the trail forks — either one may be taken. At mile 1 a side path leads to a rock outcropping. From its top look nearly straight down into the glory hole, Lake Berryessa's spillway in times of high water. Vertically tilted sandstone cliffs nose dive into Monticello Dam, and the gorge known as Devil's Gate. Engineers coveted this site for decades before Putah Creek was stilled in 1957. **THIS SITE IS DANGEROUS**. Evidence of unstable slopes is all around you, and whole hillsides have cut loose without warning. These rocks are also unusually slippery when wet. Even lug soles don't grip well. Be careful here — a fall could be fatal.

The trail takes a sharp turn to the southwest and soon tops out on Blue Ridge, covered with uniform chamise. Much of Lake Berryessa is visible. Look northwest to see Lake County's Mount Konocti, Mount Cobb and the Geysers. Devil's Gate is a wind tunnel, sometimes funnelling fog in from the Central Valley and pro-

Berryessa Dam, completed 1957

viding high speed air currents on which larger birds can hitchhike. When I was there, fog wisps gave a graphic demonstration of normally invisible air movements riding over the ridgetop, then down drafting like ghostly fiends, a hang-glider pilot's nightmare.

Turn south on level ground and pass a rock cairn in the middle of the trail. Climb a hill dotted with sandstone boulders. Blue Ridge is formed of Great Valley sedimentary rocks, which were formed in deep seas and uplifted to their present height.

At 1½ miles you are on top of the high crumbly sandstone cliff seen from below. To the east all of Stebbins Cold Canyon Reserve is in sight. Looking down into the narrow valley where Sierra Pacific Resort sits, framed by towering cliffs on all sides, it is in form, if not appearance, an alpine valley.

SUGARLOAF RIDGE STATE PARK

In the heart of the North Coast Range

DIRECTIONS: There are four ways to reach Sugarloaf by car from Napa Valley. 1) From Calistoga take Petrified Forest Road to Calistoga Road. Turn left on Highway 12 and left again on Adobe Canyon Road. It's 4 miles to the entrance kiosk. 2) From St. Helena take Spring Mountain Road to Calistoga Road. 3) From Oakville take Oakville Grade, which turns into Dry Creek Road then Trinity Road at the crest. Turn right on Highway 12 to Adobe Canyon Road. 4) From south of Napa take Highway 12 west then north to Adobe Canyon Road.

FEE: $5 per vehicle

DISTANCE: 8¾-mile loop

GRADE: Strenuous

ELEVATION GAIN: 1,500 feet

BEST TIME: Winter, spring, fall

INFO: Sugarloaf State Park, 707/833-5712

SUGGESTION: The Goodspeed Trail to Mount Hood is also highly recommended.

The headwaters of Sonoma Creek held the Wappo Indian

village of Wilikos long before the Mexicans arrived. It was a seasonal hunting camp, too cold and wet for the winter months. The Wappo were so successful in resisting the Mexican soldiers that colony attempts at Santa Rosa, Fulton and Petaluma were abandoned. In the late 1830s Wappo population dwindled as American settlers took their land and epidemic diseases took a heavy toll. In the 1850s the remaining Wappo were forcibly relocated to the Mendocino Indian Reservation.

In early pioneer days, no major trail crossed the southern Mayacmas Mountains between Napa and Sonoma valleys, isolating settlers and slowing development. The first to settle in the flat lands west of Sugarloaf Park was sea captain John Wilson, granted the 19,000-acre *Rancho Los Guilicos* in 1837. In 1858 he sold it to Scottish ship carpenter William Hood, who planted vineyard and built a three-story stone winery on Los Guilicos Creek. Mount Hood is named for him.

The rugged hills and thin soils around Sugarloaf supported marginal agriculture by 1870. The Luttrell family was first to claim the largest piece of bottom land and raise cattle, grow walnuts and subsistence crops. Later owners manufactured charcoal from oak wood between 1905 and 1910. In this era the Reynolds family built the main ranch house and the main access road through Adobe Canyon, supplanting the Nunn's Canyon road from the south.

In 1920 new owner John Warboys sold this parcel to the State of California. They planned to dam the waters of Sonoma Creek watershed, and pipe it to Sonoma State Home at Eldridge near Glen Ellen. Plans were already underway when surrounding landowners raised objections and a water rights dispute arose, suspending construction. After fifteen years the issue was settled when Sonoma Home built a dam near Eldridge. The state hospital, however, continued use of the site as a Scout camp for patients until World War II. In the 1950s the state leased it to Raffo Brothers Milk Transportation Company for cattle grazing until it became the first parcel included in Sugarloaf Ridge State Park in the early 1960s.

Other properties in the surrounding hills were used for cattle and crops, and increasingly, by the 1930s for hunting and weekend outings. The Bear Creek Ranch in the extreme northwest corner of the park, was homesteaded by the Hurd family of Saint Helena by 1914. It was a marginal operation at best. By the 1930s a Napa County group ran a hunting camp here, their only access a rough fire road off Spring Mountain. By the 1960s a new owner obtained access through the park. The ranch house burned in 1967, purportedly occupied at the time by a large group of hippies. The property was included in the state park by 1972.

Sugarloaf Ridge State Park has grown today to more than 2,700 acres, with twenty-five miles of hiking trails. Fifty primitive camp sites are offered, including a group camp that holds a hundred people. The park's location in the Coast Range is in a transitional zone between the cool, moist coastal air and dry inland air. Several distinct habitats are thus found in close proximity: redwood forest, oak woodland, mixed evergreen forest and chaparral. Wildlife remains abundant, with recent sightings of wild turkey, bobcat, mountain lion and wild pig. Some of the best trails in the park are the newest, like the Goodspeed and Brushy Peaks trails.

TRAIL NOTES:

The following loop lets you experience the heart of Sugarloaf Park. From the gentle waters of Sonoma Creek to windy ridgetop views encompassing more than half a dozen counties, you will see nearly all this area has to offer. At a fast clip this trail can be done in a few hours, but to thoroughly enjoy it, allow three-quarters of a day.

Find the trailhead for the Meadow Trail next to an interpretive display at the main parking lot. Immediately there is a connector trail to Bald Mountain Trail — stay right. The meadow on your left often holds grazing deer. To the west is Mount Hood. This watershed holds two Bald Mountains within two air miles of each other. To the southeast is Bald

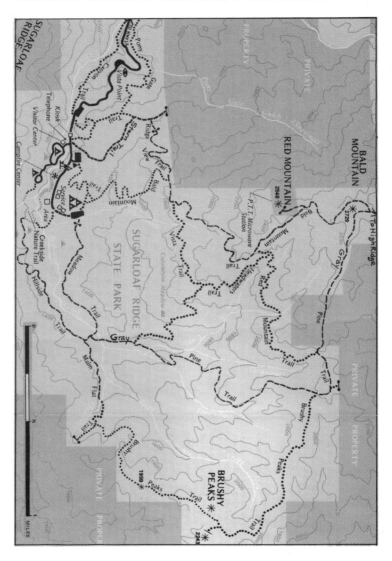

Mountain (2,275 feet, sometimes called Little Bald Mountain), just outside the park boundary. To the north is the better known Bald Mountain (2,729 feet), the one you will climb today.

Pass through a zone of chaparral and come to an even larger expanse of meadow. At ⅓ mile the Lower Bald Mountain Trail splits left. Bear to the right on the Meadow Trail. Descend to the Group Camp at ½ mile. This site features everything, including a horse corral and two stone barbecues with a crossbar spit for roasting meat. An alternate paved route ends here. Go past the metal gate across a small creek and onto the dirt road. After winter rains this is a great place to look for animal tracks such as deer and raccoon.

An expansive meadow to the right is punctuated by a single enormous coast live oak. As the meadow ends beyond ¾ mile you walk under tall bay and alder along Sonoma Creek. On the left is a bay tree seventy feet high with ten separate trunks up to two feet in diameter.

There is a wonderful picnic site at mile 1. Towering over a picnic table by the creek is a maple so large I once mistook it for an oak in its dormant stage. Cross the bridge over Sonoma Creek and at 1⅓ miles come to the Gray Pine Trail junction. Stay right on Meadow Trail. Soon there is another junction. Meadow Trail continues along the road as Hillside Trail. You turn left onto Brushy Peaks Trail.

The wide trail now follows the Malm Fork of Sonoma Creek. The trail starts to climb steeply around 1¾ miles. Behind you will appear (Sugarloaf Park's) Bald Mountain and Red Mountain. At a confusing unmarked junction, a fallen madrone tree blocks the right fork. Stay left and the trail soon narrows. The trail switchbacks in big low angle sweeps up a steep hill through mature madrone/Douglas fir forest. Below is the Malm Fork, now a vertiginous drop.

Come out into the sunlight at mile 2 with a view back to where you started. As you approach the headwaters of Malm Fork there are extensive views of the Sonoma/Napa ridge line. Before 2¾ miles you arrive at a beautifully placed grassy hillside with coast live oaks. Here at the dividing line between Sonoma Creek watershed and Dry Creek watershed must be one of the ultimate picnic sites. If someone wrote "Best Places to Make Love in California" this would be at the top of the list. Views all the way down Dry Creek take your eyes to Mount Veeder, the city of Napa and San Pablo Bay.

Turn left as you are now at the south boundary of the park. The terrain changes dramatically to chamise and manzanita and the trail turns into a steep, rocky fire road. Mount St. John (2,375 feet) is to the east. One former owner was Judge Hastings, who founded Hastings Law School. A large portion is now owned by movie director Francis Ford Coppola. The fire road sweeps up and down in giant roller coaster dips that unfortunately cannot be enjoyed at a hiker's pace. Brushy Peaks is pure chaparral territory with buckbrush, toyon, scrub oak and chamise.

An unmarked trail junction appears at 3¼ miles. Those who need more uphill punishment can continue up the steep

Looking across the slopes of Bald Mountain to Mount St. John

fire road to the top of Brushy Peak. Most will want to take the right fork, a level trail through a chaparral tunnel to a trail sign. Both trails lead to the same place. Turn right and shortly come to another junction. To the right a trail leads to Peak 2,243 — you take the not obvious left fork northeast through brush.

Reach the ridgetop at 3¾ miles for the best views of Napa Valley on this trail. The view of Saint Helena is particularly good, and many residents of the town will be able to see their own house with good binoculars. Turn sharply left at a metal stake. Hikers will make good time as they pick up the road again, while new plant species appear like chaparral pea and pearly everlasting. At mile 4 the road starts to roller coaster again. Chaparral is punctuated by groves of deciduous oaks.

At 4⅝ miles pass under high voltage power lines that march through Napa and Sonoma valleys. Fire has been a stranger here lately, indicated by thick-trunked chamise to six feet tall. The Brushy Peaks Trail ends at 4¾ miles and you continue on the Gray Pine Trail to the right. Soon you pass a private road whose owners make the point with two gates.

Larger black oaks appear, and smaller madrone and bay. At mile 5 you'll see in a window through the trees, vineyard-terraced Spring Mountain near Saint Helena. A steep hill leads to the Red Mountain Trail junction. Stay on the fire road passing an old manzanita twelve feet tall. In the spring bush lupine will be flowering. After relentless uphill, emerge onto the first meadows that stretch to Bald Mountain. On your right is a superb black oak forest that continues nearly to the mountain top.

The last uphill of the trail ends on the bald flats of Bald Mountain. Two interpretive displays locate and give mileage to thirty peaks and landmarks in the region, including Pyramid Peak 129 miles east in the Sierra. I talked with a mountain biker here who took forty minutes to gain the top from the Bald Mountain trailhead. Many bikers return by loop via Gray Pine Trail.

The downward-bound trail takes a big sweep around the hilltop, passing the High Ridge Trail, which dead-ends after a mile and a half at the old Hurd homestead. The Bald Mountain Trail passes serpentine rock outcrops and erosion gullies until meeting a paved road beyond 6¼ miles. The right fork leads to the microwave towers atop Red Mountain. Go left, passing a picnic table at 6½ miles. The roadside is alive with wildflowers in spring. The Red Mountain Trail veers off left and downhill. To the south you can see the ridge carrying Brushy Peaks Trail and realize you have circumscribed the entire watershed in a giant crescent or horseshoe.

A bench for resting is at mile 7. Descend another ⅓ mile to pass spring-fed sword ferns. Just beyond is a lovely vernal pool in an area closed for renovation. On my approach I mistook a tree frog cacophony for bull frogs. They were loud enough to record on my little battery-run Sony from one hundred feet away! Circle the pool and come to the Vista Trail junction. A rest bench at 7¾ miles marks the lower Bald Mountain Trail. This is a good shortcut to the trailhead if you have an appointment to keep.

Continue steeply down the paved road past large bosses of polished green serpentine. There is an interesting blend of chaparral and woodland species past a hairpin turn at mile 8. In ¼ mile pass a gate. Your loop continues as Stern Trail, now gravelled. A road also goes north but soon ends in private property. The Pony Gate Trail junction appears at 8⅜ miles. To your left are massive erosion gullies. Now it's clear why the road was routed away from this chronically unstable slope. Late in the day I was able to photograph a dozen deer grazing contentedly as cows in these meadows. At a junction you have the choice of heading straight to the road or continuing on trail through meadows to the parking lot at 8¾ miles.

BLUE RIDGE

Eastern edge of the North Coast Range

DIRECTIONS: From Napa take Highway 12 to Interstate 80, then I-505 to Winters, or from Rutherford take Highway 128 to Winters. Continue north on I-505 ten miles, then turn west on Highway 16. Drive 30 miles through rural Capay Valley to *lower* Yolo County Park.

An alternate scenic route goes north on Highway 29 past Clearlake Oaks. Turn right (east) on Highway 20 then south on Highway 16 ten miles to *lower* Yolo County Park.

After turning off the highway, veer left. If the gate is closed for winter, park nearby. If open, continue on County Road 40 (Rayhouse Road) then head down to the creek, cross the low-water concrete bridge and park in a small lot at the first junction. Now on foot, turn off Road 40 onto an access road that leads to group camping. The north trailhead starts at the Ada Merhoff stone memorial next to two Bureau of Land Management (BLM) trail markers.

DISTANCE: 8½ miles one way
GRADE: Strenuous
ELEVATION GAIN: 2,000+ feet
BEST TIME: Spring
INFO: Bureau of Land Management, 707/468-4000

SUGGESTIONS: Many hikers will find attaining the ridge a satisfying destination. From the top at mile 3 a volunteer trail leads to a spectacular overlook. Continuing on the main trail another mile takes you to Peak 2,868.

The round trip of nearly 17 miles can be done in a long day. The best way, though, is to hike it one way from south to north. If County Road 40 is open, car pool or have someone drop you at Fiske Creek trailhead. That way you avoid the 2,000-foot gain at the start.

Blue Ridge was named for the bluish cast of the blue oaks and chaparral on its west slope. These mountains were Patwin Indian territory, a non-agrarian tribe of traders whose routes followed Putah and Cache creeks to the coastal valleys and the sea. Trapper Ewing Young camped in Capay Valley in 1832 (Kaipai means "stream" in Patwin). He named the stream Cache Creek for the cache of goods his party stored here. The very next year flooding in the Central Valley created a malaria epidemic that killed three quarters of the Patwin nation.

The Patwins' troubles increased in 1836 when an alliance was formed between Commander Vallejo of the Sonoma garrison and Solano, the powerful Suisun chief. Solano agreed not to molest Mexican settlers in Sonoma and Napa in exchange for help in subduing his enemies. The few Patwin survivors were relocated to rancherias. One in Capay Valley still exists.

A few large ranchos were formed in the 1840s, notably by Demesio, Santiago and Francisco Berryessa in upper Capay Valley, and by naturalized citizen William Gordon. The Gordon Ranch was a well-known and popular rendezvous for settlers and hunters. It was the site of a stopover for the Bear Flag Party coming from John C. Fremont's Feather River camp in June 1846. They recruited another member and continued on through Tully Canyon to Berryessa, Pope and Napa valleys, eventually capturing the Sonoma garrison and declaring California a republic on June 14, 1846.

The 1850s saw general settlement of Capay Valley. The mountains, though, were rugged and saw sparse development. Charles F. Reed, a West Point civil engineer who earlier surveyed the town of Knight's Landing, opened a quicksilver mine near Little Blue Ridge on Davis Creek in the 1860s. The railroad pushed as far as the hamlet of Rumsey in upper Capay Valley by 1888, but fond plans of extending it through Cache Creek canyon to Lake County never materialized.

In 1906 on Cache Creek occurred one of the greatest land slides in California history, but its significance was lost due to the 8.25 magnitude earthquake that struck San Francisco only thirteen days earlier. The slide happened on May 1, 1906, near Crack Canyon, a tributary of Cache Creek. Residents downstream in Capay Valley noticed the creek level had dropped five feet overnight, but the

Mariposa lily

slide area was so inaccessible that it was two days before the cause could be confirmed. The slide that completely blocked Cache Creek was one hundred feet high and 500 feet wide on top, impounding 12,000 acre-feet of water in a lake four miles long.

Residents in Capay Valley evacuated and camped in the hills. They waited five days until the creek broke the dam, when the flood with its debris devastated the town of

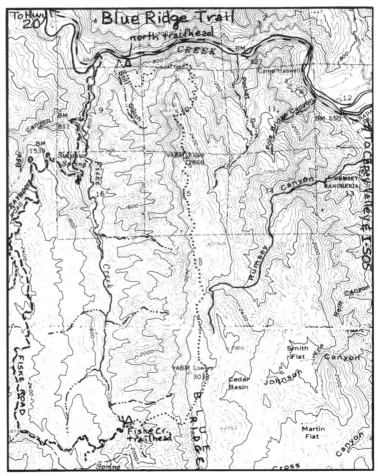

Rumsey. No one was killed or injured. The disaster in San Francisco overshadowed this event, which quickly faded into obscurity. Geologists today say that the quake (as well as heavy rainfall that winter) could easily have been a factor in the slide. The highly fractured and jointed mudstones, shales, conglomerates and sandstones in Cache Creek Canyon will continue to produce large and small landslides in the future.

Capay Valley's orchards and open fields today make it an agricultural oasis untouched by urban encroachment. Since the advent of the automobile, Cache Creek Canyon has been a popular motor outing in the spring when hundreds of native western redbud trees are in bloom. Campers, fishermen, hunters and white water rafters frequent this area too. Since the mid-1980s and the creation of the Blue Ridge Trail, hiking has become more popular. The Bureau of Land Management has been actively improving the trail for several years. Its best features are its remoteness, abundant wildlife and spring wildflowers, and outstanding views.

TRAIL NOTES:

Blue Ridge Trail has three distinct personalities. The first 2 steep miles of trail are the prettiest, partially shaded by mixed evergreen forest and highlighted with many wildflowers. The third mile, definitely the toughest of the trip, is even more steep with poor footing, many switchbacks and overgrown with chamise. With most of the climbing over, the last 5 or 6 miles of trail is an unending swath through monotonous chaparral, saved by its superb 360 degree views and decorated, to the end, with wildflowers in spring.

The trail shows you its teeth from the start, climbing steeply through a mix of oak, buckeye and gray pine, with a stunning display of wildflowers like paintbrush, brodiaea, mariposa lily and golden fairy lantern. Before ¼ mile the trail really starts to climb, following a small creek. On

Glasscock Mountain to the north, entire hillsides of chamise will be a riot of bloom in May.

At ½ mile pass under a buckeye tree, cross the creek and traverse the opposite hillside with the first major views of Cache Creek Canyon to the northwest. Another sharp turn at ¾ mile brings you face to face with your main challenge, the prominent 2,000 foot uplift seen from the highway. Unmaintained, this trail would be a poison oak gauntlet. Cross a creek scoured wide by the 1995 floods at 1¼ miles and make your only foray of the hike into grassland. The trail can get unreasonably steep at 1½ miles. Look for the white blooms of prickly poppies in late May.

Around mile 2 you climb from north-facing wooded hillsides to east-facing brushy slopes, with views of upper Capay Valley. The uniform chamise is interrupted only by an occasional ceanothus, gray pine, chaparral pea or monkeyflower. The next mile would be gruesome on a hot summer day. Keep an eye out for ticks, including the tiny lyme disease-carrying, red-bodied *Ixodes pacifica*.

Near the ridgetop at 3 miles is an unmarked junction. The right fork is a volunteer trail leading shortly to a view straight down the great uplift you have climbed. If the Central Valley is clear you'll see the Sierra Nevada Range to the east. To the west are Little Blue Ridge, Cobb Mountain and, a little south of that, Mount St. Helena. Take the left fork to continue on Blue Ridge.

A gradual climb leads to Peak 2,868 at mile 4, where you can sign the summit register enclosed in a tin can. Follow an indistinct path along the ridge, highlighted by Indian paintbrush in the spring, until the trail becomes obvious again in the chaparral. The trail is fairly level and open through miles 5 and 6.

Occasional fire rings on the trail itself show the limited camping possibilities. Lower Capay Valley is now in view. After a descent, a notch in the ridge signifies the head of Rumsey Canyon as you near mile 7. The scent of myriad blue blossom California lilac in the spring makes this loca-

Blue Ridge

tion a wild garden. Begin the ascent to Peak 3,038. The summit bench mark is off the main trail. You may notice a low profile green dome to the east — this is a water source for wildlife placed by BLM. To the west is Rayhouse Road (Road 40) a seasonal road that leads to Lake County. The trail abruptly abandons the ridge and heads steeply down to reach Fiske Creek trailhead at 8½ miles.

BALDY MOUNTAIN

This seldom-visited area offers solitude

DIRECTIONS: From Calistoga take Highway 29 past the town of Clearlake to Highway 20 and turn east. Go north at the junction of Bear Valley Road (Wilbur Springs turnoff) to the north end of Bear Valley. Turn left (west) on Brim Road (Bartlett Springs), 2.7 miles to the Walker Ridge Road junction. It's another 2.8 miles to the trailhead at the northeast corner of Indian Valley Reservoir. Look for a Bureau of Land Management (BLM) marker with the hiker symbol. The trail starts at a second BLM marker on the side road.

An alternate road for sturdy vehicles is Walker Ridge Road off Highway 20. It is 15.5 miles from Highway 20 to Bartlett Springs Road.

From the Central Valley, take Interstate 5 to Williams, turn west on Highway 20 to Bear Valley Road.

DISTANCE: 4¼ miles one way

GRADE: Strenuous

ELEVATION GAIN: 1,900 feet

BEST TIME: Winter, spring only. Summer will likely be blazing hot and dry.

INFO: Bureau of Land Management, 707/468-4000

WARNINGS: Be aware this is not the easiest trail to follow.

It is indistinct and confusing in places and you may get derailed temporarily. Don't worry. Remember two things: You *will* get to the top eventually *and* your route-finding skills will be finely honed in the process.

SUGGESTIONS: Indian Valley Brodiaea A.C.E.C. (Area of Critical Environmental Concern) holds the entire distribution of this wildflower species.

Bear Valley offers one of California's finest wildflower displays in spring.

Great numbers of American Indians called Patwin lived in the valley west of Baldy Mountain, and it came to be known simply as Indian Valley. The Patwin are the southernmost tribe of the Wintun linguistic group, who influenced greatly the Kuksu religion, a spirit-impersonating belief system in which initiates were formally indoctrinated. Many Patwin people were lured to the mission at Sonoma in 1823.

Settlement of Indian Valley by whites was slow. Poor soil overlain by stream-borne gravel deposits made agriculture a marginal business. By 1870 people like Frank Kowalski, Thomas Zimory, John Wilson, Henry Catenburg and Joseph Byron Stanton ran cattle and tried to grow fruit and nut trees. Although many of them had moved on by 1910, they left their names to the canyons, creeks and glades of the region.

Over to the east of Baldy Mountain, Brutus Epperson of Bear Valley saw a business opportunity. Hot springs like Bartlett Springs were doing well, but the only access was from Clear Lake. He formed the Bartlett Springs and Bear Valley Toll Road Company in 1873 to bring visitors from the Central Valley. Chinese built the road in only four months, and that first summer stages carried 600 passengers from Colusa, via the Leesville Road through Bear

Valley (where the toll station was), over Baldy Mountain into Indian Valley and on to Bartlett Springs.

Those anxious to avoid the toll soon built the Brim Grade Road through Complexion Canyon (the present road). Epperson, anxious to collect toll, relocated his toll station several times before settling at Barkerville at the northwest corner of Indian Valley. The proprietor, Ephraim Barker, and his wife formed a town of their own by siring twenty-two children, nineteen of whom lived on the ranch. A school was opened in Indian Valley in 1884 but falling population closed it in 1894. Two years later, Epperson's toll road went public when he sold it to the county.

The possibility of a dam in Indian Valley had been discussed as early as 1915. Yolo County farming interests were successful in completing the earthen dam on the North Fork of Cache Creek by 1974. The six-mile-long lake is used mainly for irrigation water, but also for fishing, boating and swimming. There is a small resort on the south end. Blue

Early hot springs resorts

Several hot springs resorts such as Hough Springs and Allen Springs, located on the Bear Valley/ Bartlett Springs road did good business in the 1880s and 1890s. Bartlett Springs, though, was in a class by itself, and became a world famous destination. In 1870 Napa resident Greene Bartlett was near death, legend says, when he was effected a miraculous cure by drinking these waters. It was soon a rustic resort for the seriously ill. In 1877 business partner Sam McMahon began to attract recreational visitors. A toll road was built from Nice/ Lucerne on Clear Lake, while a steamer service brought visitors across the lake from Lakeport.

By 1894 Bartlett Springs was called one of the finest natural sanitariums in the world. Five hotels accommodated up to 1,000 guests, attended by 250 employees. A small city built

Oak, Wintun and Barrel Springs camps, primitive sites found on or near Walker Ridge Road east of the lake, are free.

Baldy Mountain trail itself was first built by Department of Fish and Game as a hunter-access trail, then forgotten. Recently BLM improved it and now it is used occasionally by adventuresome hikers.

TRAIL NOTES:

The rocky trail starts straight uphill. The surrounding plant community is dominated by just a few species: cypress, manzanita and gray pine. After ⅓ mile you top the first hill. Your objective, Baldy Mountain is seen to the southeast. Indian Valley Reservoir stretches to the south, with its many drowned trees looking like a graveyard.

Soon you'll descend into a pretty creek canyon. You approach the bottom of the hill at ⅔ mile as the trail takes two switchbacks. The second one is easy to miss. Take a

up around it. For entertainment guests were provided a casino, bowling alley, ballroom, concert hall, tennis courts, golf, shuffleboard, croquet, billiards, horseback riding, swimming and, later, hiking trails. Bartlett had its own post office, Wells Fargo office, meat market and general merchandise store. The centerpiece was an open air pavilion built over the original springs. Bartlett Springs attracted the wealthy, the famous, senators, congressmen, governors and once the Queen of Rumania. It was used as a training camp by boxer "Gentleman Jim" Corbett, preparing for his big fight with John L. Sullivan.

Fire destroyed the county landmark in 1934. The open air pavilion survived, and water was still bottled, but the resort was never rebuilt. In the 1980s Vittel of France bought the resort, but despite a major marketing campaign and plans to rebuild, the enterprise failed.

sharp right-angle turn at a good size gray pine and head southeast to the creek. At ¾ mile the trail crosses the creek bed near the confluence of two steams. At the exact confluence a cypress tree separates the two streams. In February the tree will be in bloom. At a touch, pollen will fly off in a delicate yellow cloud that means suffering for the hay fever prone. After crossing, find the trail on the right side of a small clearing and head straight uphill.

Cross two creeklets and top out at 1 mile. Traverse the shoulder of the second hilltop. Gray pine, cypress and manzanita are still dominant. Look for occasional lines of stones marking the path edge.

An unsigned trail junction appears at 1¼ miles. A line of stones across your path indicates the trail turns right (the apparently larger left fork goes nowhere). For the next ½ mile the path will be vague at times. In general head south, paralleling the lake.

At 1¾ miles look for a rock cairn as you start to drop into the next canyon. Soon the trail turns east to parallel the creek. At the creek bed crossing is a single silktassel bush. Go steeply uphill and directly away from the lake (east).

Let occasional rock cairns and trail periphery stones guide you in the vicinity of mile 2. Mounts Cobb and Hannah in southern Lake County come into view, then the volcano of Mount Konocti. Soon after, the higher summits of Saint John Mountain (6,743 feet) and Snow Mountain (7,056 feet) appear to the northwest. They will be snow covered in winter.

You come to the top of a third hill beyond 2¼ miles. At a confusing section, traverse down and left to a pronounced notch. Here is a remarkable change in vegetation. In a single step you finally leave the gray pine/manzanita community and walk into almost solid chamise. The sudden transition is effective for several hundred yards in either direction. They say nature abhors a straight line, but God signed the veto on this bill.

From the notch, climb again through dense, head-high

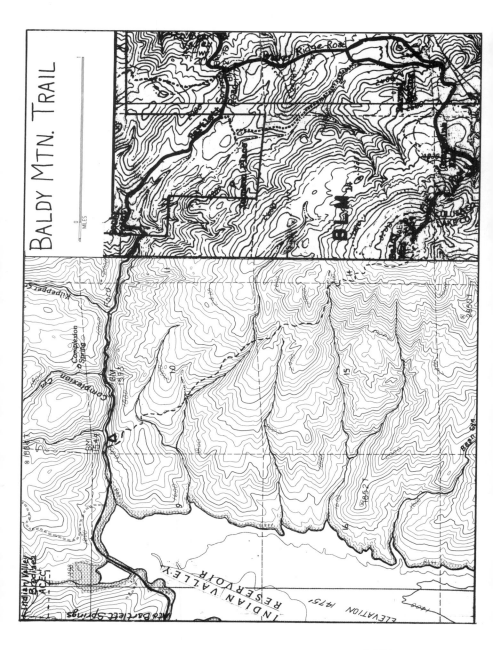

BALDY MTN. TRAIL

Baldy Mountain's straight-line vegetation change

chamise and some scrub oak and buckbrush. Look for exposures of rock called pencil slate, splintered into thousands of fragments, some only one-eighth inch wide.

You are now embarking on perhaps the most frustrating part of the trail. At many of the switchback turns it will be unclear which way to go. Explore options to find the right one. If you find yourself lost in the chaparral, sliding off a thirty degree hillside into sharp-thorned buckbrush, as I did, STOP! Don't panic. Cuss a little, then calmly retrace your steps to the last spot you know was a real trail. Most likely, a turn in the trail was missed.

At around 2¾ miles the trail stops switchbacking and heads directly to the top of a knoll. Continue along the poorly cut ridge trail. The trail turns southeast and heads downhill, and in another 500 feet passes a respectable scrub oak in a creek bed.

The terrain soon changes to cypress forest as you approach the north shoulder of Baldy Mountain at 3¼ miles. From here views east should be excellent on clear days, with nothing between you and the Sierra Nevada.

As the well defined trail ascends gradually, the next ½ mile becomes a delight. A knobcone pine forest, with trees to thirty-five feet high, is a pleasure to walk through. This north-facing hillside holds more moisture, evident in the appearance of bay and the size of the oak leaves.

Evergreen oaks appear as the knobcone forest thins. At 3¾ miles you leave the protection of the forest and enter chaparral habitat showing burn scars. Indian Valley Reservoir is now much farther below than when last seen. Come around the shoulder of the last hill at mile 4, with the summit within easy reach. You may see high flying geese returning to wetlands in the Central Valley. If there is tule fog in the valley, they must use their own brand of radar to find their destination.

At 4¼ miles you reach the somewhat anticlimactic top of Baldy Mountain. A hollow pipe in the ground surrounded by rocks marks the 3,409-foot summit. Just beyond is the first trail marker since the start and a fire road that descends to Walker Ridge Road. On a clear day snow-covered Mount Lassen will be visible astride the Sierra/Cascade crest.

SUGGESTED READING

Calkins, Victoria, *The Wappo People*, Pileated Press, Santa Rosa, California, 1994.

Grieg, Jack R., *The Vessels of the Napa River*, Napa County Historical Society (from *Gleanings*), Napa, California, 1984.

Griffiths, Edith R., *Exploration For Oil in Berryessa Valley*, Napa County Historical Society (from *Gleanings*), Napa, 1970.

Lange, Dorothea and Pirkle Jones, *Death of a Valley*, Aperture, Inc., New York, 1960.

Lyman, W.W. Jr., *The Lyman Family*, Napa County Historical Society, (from *Gleanings*), Napa, 1980.

Manson, Michael W., *Landslide and Flood Potential Along Cache Creek*, adapted from *Landslide Hazards along Cache Creek between Clear Lake and Capay Valley, Lake, Colusa, and Yolo counties*, California Division of Mines and Geology Open-File Report 89-30, May, 1990.

Mattison, Elise, *California's Fossil Forest of Sonoma County*, from *California Geology*, September, 1990.

McKenzie, Robert E., *The Monticello Rodeo and Barbecue*, Napa County Historical Society (from *Gleanings*), Napa, 1975.

Neelands, Barbara, *Reason Tucker, The Quiet Pioneer*, Napa County Historical Society (from *Gleanings*), Napa, 1989.

Stanton, Ken, *Mount St. Helena and Robert Louis Stevenson State Park, a history and guide*, Bonnie View Books, Saint Helena, California, 1993.

Stevenson, Robert Louis, *The Silverado Squatters*, Lewis Osborne, Ashland, Oregon, 1974,

Stewart, George Rippey Jr., *Stevenson in California, A Critical Study*, Master's Thesis, University of California, Berkeley, 1920.

Tortorolo, Mario J., *History of the City of Napa Water Supply*, Napa County Historical Society, (from *Gleanings*), Napa, 1978.

Verardo, Jennie and Denzil, *Dr. Edward Turner Bale and His Grist Mill*, Napa County Historical Society, (from *Gleanings*), Napa, 1979.

Walters and Larkey, *Yolo County, Land of Changing Patterns*, Windsor Press, Windsor, California, 1987.

Wichels, John, *There is the Yountville Camp Grounds, So What?*, Napa County Historical Society, Napa, 1982.

INDEX

ABOUT THE AUTHOR

Ken's long-standing interest in the outdoors, which includes hiking, backpacking and mountaineering in the western United States and Canada, is perhaps a direct result of growing up in the concrete confines of Los Angeles. He has lived and worked in Napa Valley for some fifteen years. His first book, *Mount St. Helena and Robert Louis Stevenson State Park, a history and guide*, was published in 1993.